BUDGETING

Managing Personal Income for the Average Person

(Gaining Financial Freedom in an Easy to Follow System That Will Change)

Danny Jones

Published by Alex Howard

Danny Jones

All Rights Reserved

ISBN 978-1-77485-062-6

Legal & Disclaimer

Table of Contents

Introduction

Have you been struggling with your finances and find yourself living from paycheck to paycheck?

Are you tired of working so hard yet not living the kind of life you want?

Do you want to know how to manage your money effectively to achieve financial freedom?

If you do, you are in the right place.

If you work really hard, the chances are that you dedicate about 40 hours of your time every week to work, be productive, and earn a living. And that does not include the time you use to prepare to go to work, the time you spend while commuting, or having coffee breaks or the free hours that are lost because you are exhausted from working all day.

If you are willing to dedicate all that time of your productive years to earn a living, then you owe it to yourself to ensure that what you earn is properly utilized in the things that you hold dear most.

This is where a budget comes into play. It enables you to track all your expenditure, however big or small. It helps you discover how much money you spend on everything from lunch breaks and gasoline to clothing, groceries, entertainment, etcetera. An understanding of your expenditure enables you to allocate money to what is most important to you, and avoid spending money on things that are not as important, and this is what you will learn in this book.

In this book, you will learn what exactly budgeting entails, how to come up with a suitable budget that suits your lifestyle, ways of ensuring that you stick to the budget you have set, and how to make changes to your budget.

I hope you enjoy it!

Chapter 1: Why Budget?

Financial control

Money should never control you; it should be the other way around. When money controls you, you tend to live a one-day-millionaire's life characterized by extravagance and orientation to the present. Because money tells you that you earn it to spend it, you commonly find yourself stressed, wondering where your money went to, and in debt.

On the contrary, if you control your money, you won't be living the kind of life reminiscent of a millionaire, but you save yourself from stress, worry, and debt. The financial control means that before you even touch your money, you know where it's supposed to go, how you're supposed to spend it, and when you'll spend it. This is where the budget comes in.

Financial tracker

Count how many times you've thought about not knowing where your money went. Count the number of times when you got shocked that your money's almost gone. Count the number of times when that money supposedly for your savings account was used anyway. During those times, you probably have felt as though you still have enough on your account.

When it comes to money, it is easy to commit calculation errors, and sometimes, these errors can be fatal. If you miss a payment, you'll get hit with fees; and when that happens, you'll find it difficult to recover. Budgeting helps you track how you spend your money, and as it gets depleted, you'll know how to strategize your spending.

Financial goals

Have you ever been overwhelmed with the desire to possess something the first time you laid eyes on it? Have you ever been tempted to get it because you had the money? If not, how soon were you able to get it? And how did you eventually get it? These questions point to the simple goal-setting methods we employ helps us stabilize our budget.

In contrast to what most people believe, we are establishing a goal when creating a budget. And because the amount of money we wish to spend on something becomes the goal, we make compromises. For example, we might opt to forego buying a new smartphone so we can finally take home an HD television.

Financial striving

Budget not only tells us how much money we have. It also tells us how much money we need to raise. In ordinary conversations, we call this the act of "making ends meet." What if we don't have enough to make those ends meet? This is where the power of budgeting benefits us.

Just like compromising, budgeting tells us whether or not we need to work more, or whether or not we need to look for other sources of income. Because we know that budgeting is goal-setting in itself, we can see how our long-term financial plans are coming along. We can also see how we can make adjustments to our short-term goals to make our money just enough to make such ends meet.

Financial health

Budget reveals three things: how much money we have, how much money we need, and how much money we can still save. By looking at these aspects, we're able to analyze how we our finances are. We also come to know how good we are at making money, at spending money, and at saving money. Financial health doesn't mean financial freedom. In fact, financial freedom is a myth because even billionaires benefit more if they live on a budget. Financial health then refers to how we appraise our financial condition. Hence, it is highly subjective. Some of us might say that our budget adequately reflects our financial wellness while others

may say that they need to do more for
their budget to be effective.

Chapter 2: Budgeting Basics

Regardless of what method you use to budget, you will need to understand some basic concepts that must be used. These tools and concepts are vitally important to your budgeting success. They should be used diligently, especially when you are just starting out. You will need to use the information from these tools to help you create effective and accurate budgets.

Tracking Income

There are some important things to keep in mind when tracking income. You want your budget to be as accurate as possible. If you overestimate how much income you will have you could throw your entire budget off balance. You could wind up short for the week or month, and be unable to pay an important bill.

When you consider your income for your budget you should calculate all **reliable** sources of income. This means that you need to incorporate only that income which is guaranteed. This is usually your paycheck. When you calculate the money you will have, don't use your gross pay. If you work the same number of hours per week you can use the net pay from your check stubs to see what you can budget for income. If your work hours vary, calculate your gross income and deduct 25% for taxes. You may have fewer deductions than that, but it is better to be safe than sorry.

You may have other sources of income such as that from a side job, child support or alimony. If you have steady income from one or more of these sources that is guaranteed, feel free to add it to your budgeted income. Guaranteed income is income that is received on a scheduled basis. It also must be received with continuity, such as on time each period for at least three to six months.

If you have a child support or alimony order but the money doesn't always come on time or at all, you should not count it as income in your budget. If you budget for this income and then it doesn't show up it will throw your entire financial plan out of whack and you will have to face potentially serious consequences.

Tracking Expenses

There are many ways that you can track your expenses and spending. Tracking expenses is especially important when you first start budgeting. It is vital that you know where all of your money is going. Creating a budget of what you anticipate spending is an important aspect of your budget. But tracking expenses tells you where your money is actually going.

Tracking expenses is important because it helps you determine what you need to budget for. Bills like rent and a car payment are fixed expenses that you don't really have to think about. But most expenses are variable, meaning that they are different each month. The only way to budget for variable expenses is to have some idea of what that amount might be.

It is pretty easy to track your expenses. You can easily create a spreadsheet on your computer where you can enter your expenses daily and have a monthly total running at the bottom. There are such spreadsheets available online as well. This requires keeping receipts and entering each expense.

You can also get expense trackers on your smart phone with many different available apps. This is helpful for making sure that you don't miss any expenses when you enter them into your tracking at home. If you are single you can just use the expense tracker app. If you have a significant other you will need to combine your tracking and theirs on a master spreadsheet or software.

Budgeting for Variable Expenses

This is where your expense tracker will come in handy. When you track your spending for the previous month you can use that information to help you budget for your variable expenses for the following month. As you continue this trend you can calculate the average spending for that item based on several months of data. This will give you the most accurate budget possible.

It is important that you give yourself some leeway when it comes to variable expenses. You should always pad them, even if just by a few dollars, when doing your budget. This way you will not run into serious problems if the expense ends up being a bit more than you thought. If you have extra money at the end of the budget period because you padded your variable expenses you can use that money to help make larger purchases that you couldn't afford before, or you can add it to your savings nest egg.

It is best to budget as closely as possible. As already mentioned your expense tracker can help you with some of that. Past spending habits can help you calculate the budget for things like gasoline, food and household items. Some variable expenses require a different tactic.

For utility bills, for example, you will want to look back at your previous bills for the current season. In other words, if it is summer you need to look back to see what the average bill was in the previous summer. This can usually be done by contacting your utility company and requesting the information. If this is your first season in your home you can still contact the utility company and they will give you average utility costs for that month in the previous year based on the previous resident's usage.

Grocery Budget Tips

Budgeting for groceries is perhaps one of the most difficult variable expenses to calculate. Food prices vary greatly. Sometimes you can get great deals and catch awesome sales, and sometimes you will have to pay full price no matter where in the city you go to shop. Meat prices rise and fall. Any number of things can change the price of food with little or no notice.

Your previous spending will give you a starting point for your grocery budget. Look back through several months of spending to get an idea of the average amount you spend. Try to go with the higher number just to make sure that you have enough budgeted.

It also helps to make a meal plan for the budget period, make a grocery list, and estimate the amount of money you will spend to fulfill that list. Again, pad the budget a bit to make sure you have enough money for groceries in case prices rise or something unexpected comes up.

There is one great tool that you can use to help you make your grocery budget more accurate. You can build a spreadsheet for it. There are also a few apps and websites that will help you do this. You have to track every item that you buy. You bring home your grocery receipt and input the store, date, item, size, and price. By doing this you will be able to see exactly what you pay for each item.

When you create a meal plan for the next budget period you can look back at your itemized list and see what you paid for each item. Your grocery list will be made and you will have an almost exact dollar amount of what you will spend. Not everyone has the time to do this, but if you can it is a great tool that can really help you.

Chapter 3: How Do You Balance A Budget?

It doesn't take an act of Congress to balance your price range. You want a dedication to financial goals, willpower to stay under your approach and a willingness to make the essential adjustments.

Here are 5 ways to do it.

1. Set up your budget

Before developing a price range, evaluate your financial records. The use of bank and credit card statements becomes aware of each how lots income you take in, and how much you normally spend on expenses. Assemble the financial facts into two separate categories: predicted income and predicted costs.

Predicted earnings need to include wages, self-employment earnings, investment earnings and different resources of earnings. Next, list expected charges together with mortgage or rent, utilities, and cable and cellular telephone prices.

Lastly, subtract predicted fees from expected profits to determine the quantity you have available after fees are paid. The available amount needs to be put away for rainy days, used to pay down debt or applied to other financial desires.

2. Separate the necessities from the desires

Also separate your predicted expenses into two additional classes: discretionary charges and nondiscretionary charges. Discretionary costs are "wishes," along with entertainment, eating out or fitness center memberships. Nondiscretionary fees are requirements, together with rent, utilities, and groceries.

Evaluate discretionary charges to look at whether or not you can pick out prices that would be eliminated or decreased.

3. Tune your costs

Periodically replacing your finance to list the actual costs for every category. Compare budgeted amounts with real spending.

If you are tech-savvy, use telephone budgeting programs to help you preserve the song of charges. Or, if you revel in recording the old fashioned way, preserve a notepad to report your expenses.

4. Overview and regulate regularly

Prepare a finance at the start of every month or each pay cycle. This offers you the possibility to study your previous month's finances and identify regions in which you want to control spending. Make any adjustments necessary that will help you attain financial desires, such as saving or decreasing debt.

5. Finances for existence's pleasures

Do not forget making plans for certain indulgences, which include date nights, or a new dress or pair of footwear. Making plans ahead of time will assist you to apprehend what you may manage to pay for, and also serves as a reminder to deal with yourself once in a while.

Create balanced finances

Finances can help you:

Maintain track of your profits and fees

Live on top of your monthly bills

Be organized for surprising costs

Keep away from overspending

Determine out how a great deal you want to shop to meet your economic desires.

Five components of a budget

Profits after taxes – this is the quantity of money you need to work with each month. If you're self-employed, a seasonal or part-time worker, or paid utilizing fee, your profits might also range. To create your month-to-month price range, take your annual earnings and divide by using

12. Use this amount as your month-to-month profits.

Fixed monthly prices – these costs generally tend to live the identical (or close to the identical) from month to month. They consist of payments which include your hire or loan, cable, internet, utilities, and fixed mortgage repayments.

Variable costs – those costs exchange from month to month. They consist of things like fuel, groceries, your everyday coffee, food out and enjoyment expenses.

Occasional expenses – these costs come up every so often, such as garb, presents and holidays.

Savings – Make room on your budget for short-time period emergency savings and longer-term savings that will help you reach your economic goals.

If you're self-hired, a seasonal or component-time employee, or paid utilizing fee, your earnings can also range. To create your month-to-month finances, take your annual earnings and divide by way of 12. Use this amount as your monthly income.

Discern out your variable fees

Use affordable estimates to create your first budget. Then, tune your spending over the following couple of months. Jot down each purchase in a notebook, maintain receipts for the whole thing or create a spreadsheet. After monitoring your spending for a few months, move returned for your budget and adjust it if you want to.

Plan for occasional prices

Include room for your finances for charges that arise occasionally, inclusive of clothing, items, and vacations. Learn extra approximately making plans for occasional fees.

Budgets are for saving too

Pay yourself first – make financial savings part of your finances. Plan to have this quantity moved to a financial savings account as soon as your paycheque gets deposited. While you make it automated, it's less complicated to shop.

If you have some money left over to your finances

After you have paid the bills, upload for your financial savings. Construct an emergency fund for unexpected bills that arise (like a furnace that breaks in January). The extra you store, the earlier you'll reach your monetary goals.

Balancing Your Budget

If you're new to budgeting, your finance may not stability the first time you attempt. You ought to search for places wherein you could spend less and make adjustments alongside the way.

A way to create and control a finance

Budgeting has a horrific recognition amongst a variety of American households who view it as a manner to strip the entire laugh out of spending money. No greater purchasing. No more ingesting out at eating places. No more golfing on weekends.

That is not the purpose of a motive of a budget.

A budget shows how tons of money you have coming in and the way the one's funds are spent. It's one of the most vital gears in building a successful economic destiny, as it facilitates you get the maximum from your money.

Regardless of monetary standing or which generation you fall into, every patron can benefit from creating and handling a budget. A finance offers humans a feeling of manage over their money. Consider a finance as an economic basis. Each person's foundation goes to be exceptional, just as each monetary situation is distinct.

Choosing a Budgeting device

There are four primary approaches to create, track and monitor finances. Each device uses one of the kind strategies, but all of them center on agency and attention to element.

The notebook and Pen: this is the oldest method for budgeting, and it's also the least luxurious alternative. With this technique, you sincerely write down all your resources of income and all of your charges. If they balance, you're accurate to go.

The Spreadsheet: The most popular spreadsheet software program for budgeting is Microsoft Excel. Many websites provide free samples of Excel budgeting worksheets that consumers can use, rather than seeking to create their personal. A spreadsheet helps you to prepare a lot of data easily and does the math for you.

Free online software program: Several free net-based software packages may assist with budgeting. Such packages like Manilla and Mint.Com permit you to create and group your prices into classes and tune you're spending so that you can see exactly wherein your cash goes as quickly because the transaction takes region.

Economic software program: There also are economic software applications, but you want to be computer-savvy to apply them. Quicken is the main product.

Dave Ramsey's 0-based Budgeting: famous economic personality Dave Ramsey recommends a zero-based budgeting device where you pre-assign all your bucks at the start of the month the usage of envelopes.

You could also take a look at along with your local credit union or bank for guidelines and tricks. Your saving group can also actually have budgeting worksheets accessible to get you started. If you choose, the U.S. Financial Literacy and education fee (FLEC) has numerous budgeting worksheets and resources that will help you at any level of existence.

Creating a Budget

Budgeting Strategies and techniques range across the board. There might be differences, for example, between what works for a primary-year university pupil and one for a retiree. However, there are five simple steps in growing a finance. They're all vital due to the fact they build on each other, helping you arrange your finance sensibly.

Step 1: Set goals

You need to determine which goals cope with requirements and which of them cover luxuries. Then, you can prioritize your financial desires therefore.

Instantaneous monetary desires consist of protecting current charges. Some of these are obligatory and include your mortgage or lease charge, automobile loans, utility bills, baby care, meals, cell cellphone, and family substances. Secondary desires, called discretionary gadgets, consist of non-crucial apparel, subscriptions, dining out and taking holidays. Lengthy-variety economic dreams can also include retirement savings, investments, and charitable donations. If you have debt, paying it down may be each compulsory and discretionary. Making required payments is crucial to financial solvency, however paying debt early, while no longer required, could make long-term sense.

Step 2: Calculate your earnings and fees

Once you determine your monetary desires, you need a plan for reaching them. To try this, you want to evaluate your income and your fees. Most people budget month-to-month because maximum bills follow a month-to-month time table.

Begin through creating a list of your month-to-month income assets, including your salary (after taxes), any bonuses you incur on an ordinary basis, and baby aid or alimony bills. If you don't understand the exact quantity, you could use an estimate.

Once you have your numbers, add them up. The full is your month-to-month earnings.

The subsequent part of the equation is your charges, which fall into three classes: constantly devoted expenses, variable committed charges, and discretionary expenses.

Fixed dedicated prices: these have a hard and fast month-to-month amount, consisting of your mortgage or lease.

Variable devoted fee: This range from one month to the subsequent month primarily based on need, and would encompass groceries and gas.

Discretionary prices: As mentioned, those are non-compulsory prices and encompass undertaking and leisure. A gym membership might also fall into this category. Discretionary charges frequently make lifestyles extra gratifying, however they must be the first prices to move if you couldn't afford the fundamentals.

If you fail to repay your credit score card bills every month, you'll start to pay a terrific deal of interest. This could play havoc with any price range. If your carried-over credit score card payments consume up greater than 10% of your monthly profits, you should don't forget to speak me with a nonprofit credit counselor. Over the telephone or online, a loose credit counseling consultation will walk you through your finances and recommend fees that may be reduced or eliminated. if you qualify for a debt control program, you may be capable of lessening your month-to-month debt bills as properly.

Step 3: analyze Your Spending and stability Your Checkbook

The aim in budgeting is to make certain your charges do now not exceed your earnings. If they do, and more money goes out than is coming in, you then want to make adjustments. This doesn't always suggest you need to start penny-pinching; it's time to revisit the discretionary cost category and spot where you're inclined and able to reduce the fats.

If you make any payments by taking a look at, your checkbook sign up can help you keep the song of incoming and outgoing money, and what you invest in. Even though paying by taking a look at is turning into rarer, folks who persist with this price approach ought to maintain their checkbooks balanced. This can help you avoid overdraft costs or bounced assessments, and it may shed a few lights for your spending conduct.

Step 4: Revisit your unique finances

When you've had a chance to monitor your earnings and expenses for a month or two, you may be extra aware of regions that want adjusting. Perhaps your initial monthly income estimates had been off, or perhaps you didn't account for fees like vehicle repairs or veterinary bills. Make modifications, but usually, balance inflows with outflows.

As soon as you work out all of the kinks for your budget, you need to commit to following it. No finance is for all time, but, so periodic opinions are key to fulfillment.

If you get a merchandising, as an instance, you can boom your discretionary spending in addition to your savings goals. Then again, a layoff or fewer paintings hours could mean slicing returned on spending till you restore your profits.

Financial savings should be a part of the plan. Economic planners advocate that your financial savings cowl six months of profits, sufficient to compensate for an activity loss or other emergencies. You would possibly find it useful to open a separate savings account and fund it progressively till you attain the aim. Preserving a separate account will make it extra hard to raid the emergency fund to cover non-necessities.

Step 5: dedication

Developing a budget is an outstanding step in working closer to a greater financially sound future for you and your own family. Committing in your finances gets you there. Stay practical, evaluate it frequently and don't be afraid to alter. Budgeting is all about stability.

Managing your budget when unexpected bills Arrive

As referred to, an emergency fund is critical to monetary safety. Start with the aid of setting aside $50 consistent with week. In a yr, you'll have $2, six hundred, plus any interest, for while the fridge stops operating or when the transmission blows.

Professionals advise searching at your withholding taxes to locate hidden cash. If you acquire a massive refund each year, perhaps you need to exchange your submitting popularity to acquire extra cash on your paycheck to a position in the direction of an emergency fund. Unless this is, you're placing your tax go back budget into that fund.

Scientific crises especially can turn a balanced budget the wrong way up. Negotiate large medical charges, which include an emergency sanatorium stay, with the health center. Nearly all hospitals negotiate charges. Frequently if you touch them at once instead of ready until the amount goes into collections, the sanatorium or company's workplace can installation a payment plan.

If not, a scientific invoice consolidation may assist, as it permits you to combine all your scientific payments into one decrease monthly invoice through an organization or a financial institution mortgage. This no longer best makes it less complicated on you; however, the association protects your credit score rating because you're capable of make on-time bills. The disadvantage is it can take you longer to pay your debt in full.

Benefits of Budgeting

Everyone can benefit from taking a suggested and proactive approach to govern their budget. Committing for your finances will help manual you into a far higher economic role.

Budgeting can improve your life because it:

Well-known shows waste. Growing finances sheds light on areas that many humans forget on a day-to-day foundation.

Directs priorities. A budget permits human beings to observe the massive photo of their spending behavior and set new priorities to maximize their money's capacity.

Creates new behavior. When people get a clearer photo of ways they've been the use of their money, it lets in them to shift prices into special classes, making them greater conscious of pointless spending.

Reduces stress. Finance is one of the top strain-inducing conditions. While there is a feel of manipulating over the cash coming in and the cash going out, the stress can rework into a sense of empowerment.

Educates. Having a finance lets people view cash as a tool, moving the mind-set to attention on lengthy-time period dreams and destiny wishes.

Creating finances is step one, however, preserving the finances is where you start to see an actual increase in yourself and greater stretch on your dollar. Sticking to finances can be a difficult assignment for those who aren't used to spending barriers or strength of will of their budget, so it's crucial to hold a superb mindset in the direction of the manner.

Staying influenced can assist alleviate some of the pressures of budgeting. Consider putting aside some money every month so that you can stay up for a chilled excursion at the end of the year.

Eventually, set sensible goals. Begin slowly, building up to a plan that works for you and your lifestyle.

The Finer factors

Wants vs. Desires

"you may continually Get What You Want", one of the Rolling Stones famous Nineteen Sixties hits, touches on a difficulty a lot of us face all of the time. The message is you may not be capable of getting belongings you want, however if you strive, you'll get what you need.

How do you separate wishes from needs and why bother? For a lot of us, knowing where to attract the line can suggest the distinction between creating a successful finance and going broke. So what's the distinction. Maximum desires are synonymous with non-discretionary costs. They encompass shelter, which needs the price of rent or a mortgage, and meals, which leads to grocery payments. There are masses other items that can be basic and non-negotiable; however, the non-negotiable category leaves room for choice.

For instance, if you need an automobile to get to paintings, you can purchase a used Kia sedan or a new BMW. The price difference is massive, and the Beemer is certain to electrify your buddies and provide a great using revel in. The query is what are you able to afford? If you make a $500,000 in 12 months, the BMW is probably yours without stretching your finances. But if you're taking home $40,000, it's better to stick with the Kia.

The identical rule applies to a house – need to you lease a one-bedroom condominium or purchase a $400,000 house? Again, both offer a haven, however at radically exclusive costs.

There's also the difference among wishes and gadgets that you could get by using without. Reflect on consideration of taking a holiday to Thailand as opposed to a week driving to state parks close to your own home. Each can provide satisfying and relaxing locations to spend your downtown, however, the expenses are noticeably unique. Additionally, think about impulse buys. Say you go to domestic improvement save to buy a few lawn fertilizer and leave with a lawnmower you hadn't deliberate to buy. You might need a new mover, however it's a terrific concept to investigate fashions and charges earlier than putting your money down.

Knowing the difference between wants and desires is a key to a successful price range. You can finance for a few impulse purchases or product enhancements, however, recognize what you're doing, show restraint and usually ensure the balance of your finances.

Seasonal expenses

A giant quantity of your money is in all likelihood to go to one-off charges that rise over 12 months. Examples include vacation offers, birthday presents, summertime excursion costs, and lower back-to-faculty spending. A few seasonal expenses are for stand-alone items like offers, others are for basics. Heating your domestic is an issue for the bloodless-climate months, for instance, and a higher water bill would possibly coincide with irrigating your garden within the summertime. Clothing is also seasonal, with swimming suits for the summer and heavy jackets for the winter.

While you draw finances, examine your outflows for the duration of the past 12 months or two and estimate the effect of seasonal fees, then construct those prices into your plan. If your summer season expenses are a great deal better than springtime, ensure you store enough within the spring to fund spending inside the summertime.

Checking in for your finances

Budgets are living documents. Just as existence is continuously converting, the needs of your budget trade too. For this reason, it's properly to frequently evaluation your budget to modify for changes in income and prices.

What needs to you keep in mind? On the income aspect, you should make modifications if you get a raise or receive a windfall like an inheritance. You want to modify if you lose your activity or circulate to a new one. Getting married or divorced requires a large reworking of your budget. So does having a toddler. Now and then the modifications are smaller or transient, such things as a medical health insurance copayment would possibly require a transient adjustment.

You don't want to overtake your entire finance when adjustments occur. Your lease is rent, and what you spend each month in your vehicle is not going to change. However other things are more flexible. If your income drops, you might consume out less. If it is going up, you can keep greater, pay off debt quicker or make a discretionary buy.

There's no tough and speedy rule about when to check your finances. Some financial specialists recommend doing it continuously, others advocate every several months. It's possibly appropriate to take into account revisiting your budget when life-converting occasions occur, and set intervals to regulate for smaller stuff like inflation and modifications in fixed expenses.

Computerized saving and endorsed percentages

You should strongly don't forget making computerized saving part of your finances. What's automated saving? It's the cash you place aside for investment an emergency account, procuring Christmas items later within the 12 months or creating a college fund to your youngsters.

Computerized saving is pleasantly handled thru paycheck withholding. If you're saving for retirement and also your corporation gives a 401(k) plan, join up and have money withheld out of your paycheck. Many employers also offer medical and childcare savings plans, which can be normally tax-exempt. You can also have your salary routinely deposited in a bank account, then transfer part of the pay to a financial savings account which you don't plan to touch.

There are many techniques for automated savings. Communicate to an economic adviser to research greater about the options and what quantity of saving you can have the funds for. Once you implement a plan, stick with it. Percentages will range, however if your agency wills healthy contributions in your 401(ok), store at the least the maximum quantity a good way to be matched. Different financial savings may be largely decided by using your income and expenses. If you want to withhold 20% of your paycheck to cover the rent, make certain you do it. Knowing how much money you want and saving for it's going to ensure you meet your prices and prepare for the future.

Monetary professionals have come up with endorsed possibilities for spending to help humans budgeting for the primary time. For example, it's far advised you spend no more than 30% of your gross monthly income on housing, whether or not you're renting or owning.

Motors are the next biggest expense for purchasers and likely the biggest temptation to overspend. The satisfactory idea is to preserve spending between 10% and 15% of your monthly income. Something past that stretches you thin, mainly if an economic emergency arises.

Pupil loans might be some other variable to your monthly price range. Numerous earnings-based repayment plans restrict your payments to 10-15% of your profits. That's a secure range, however, regularly will extend bills some years and becomes costing you a small fortune in hobby fees. Try using 20% of your budget, mainly if you don't have a vehicle fee or are splitting hire with roommates.

Different suggested percentages for ongoing expenses include utilities (10%); meals (10-15%) and financial savings (10-15%).

Timing your price range

You need to decide to stay on finances until you see outcomes. The best way to perform this is to create an annual plan that covers your fixed costs like hire and car payment, your seasonal charges like vacation give and holidays and your discretionary prices like consuming out and buying clothes. Work all these things into a 12-month projection and comply with it.

If you discover flaws within the plan or your cash flow adjustments, you can modify it. Otherwise, attempt to live with it. Consider using budgeting software programs or apps that will help you. If you field yourself, you'll be surprised as debts get paid, financial savings develop and your desires are met.

How to Properly Balance a Budget

Initially... what is the definition of a "balanced price range"? You've heard the authorities get warmth for hardly ever balancing; so that you comprehend it ought to be critical. But that's simply the authorities. Do I need a balanced price range? I imply I'm handiest handling one man or woman's price range, no longer the whole international locations.

How does that make your experience? At the cease of the month, you aren't within the positives or the negatives. You are flawlessly balanced. Holy crap, a person noted something in your life as "best". Now you're on board. Ay Ay Captain!

We all realize budgets are right for maintaining bill bills, preserving finances in order, and supporting us to avoid overspend. However how exactly do I make one?

Observe my 10 simple steps, and then watch this video made by using Investopedia (because they smash it down actual pleasant).

Step 1 – what are your month-to-month profits after taxes?

Step 2 – What are your fixed charges? (ie. Rent, Utilities, coverage)

Step 3 – What are your variable expenses? (ie. Groceries, gasoline, smartphone bill)

Step 4 – How lots do you positioned closer to savings?

Step five – Insert all of the above totals right into a spreadsheet.

Step 6 – Calculations come up with an inexperienced mild or a red mild. What color is yours? If it's pink, we've got a hassle. If it's green, I have a solution.

Step 7 – If red, modify spending to stay inside your way.

Step eight – If green, congratulations! Now could be some time to pick out where those properly "expenses" go. Financial savings? Investments? Emergency fund? The world is your oyster.

Step nine - $zero general? Wow, you're higher at this than I thought.

Step 10 – Repeat steps every month to keep spend so as and reach financial desires.

I understand this might not be a home run the first time, or first few times, but right here's to hoping. Budgets and budget can regularly be overwhelming, so it's important which you discover a manner to make it amusing. Challenge yourself with a new aim each month.

Goals that you may set should usually be smart (specific, measurable, doable, practical & well-timed). Set quick, mid, and long term goals that provide you with something to sit up for at exceptional points for the duration of the 12 months, or future years.

The closing component to do not forget is that a spreadsheet won't be the quality budgeting device for you. I individually write down my prices via hand after which assessment from there because I feel a good deal extra accountable this way. You are probably maximum successful via the usage of a budgeting app or internet site. If this is your first time developing a price range, give your self-time to get secure in knowing in which you spend is going. Does it not position too much strain on you to make it faultless?

Easy approaches to stability Your finances with a purpose to Make You realize That it is nothing to fear about

Budgeting may be daunting. It's a very adult element to do, and if you're only just figuring out a way to be a person, grownup stuff like budgets can be frightening. However here's the aspect: budgeting isn't always all that frightening! Here are some matters which can be much less worrisome than budgets: weather alternate, Donald Trump, potholes in the street, now not calling your mother and father enough, binge-ingesting, the idea of friends now not being available to circulation on-line. Budgeting does not need to be something you have to fear approximately if you do it properly. And doing it properly isn't always that hard at all.

At the same time as budgeting might vary from man or woman to character, there are certain commonplace things we can all and need to do to balance our budgets. These things are so easy too, so you don't have to be an accountant to get the grasp of it. And when you begin doing these clean matters, you may start to recognize that things like budgeting sincerely are not that hard to do and that you should not fear a lot. Perhaps you might not be able to splurge on that cashmere sweater this month, but hey, at least you may be able to pay rent! Here are some smooth methods to balance your finances to make you realize it's not anything to fear about.

1. Placed financial savings In A one-of-a-kind Account, without delay

As soon as you receive a commission, positioned a portion of it into savings but that tons are is up to you, but make it consistent and make it immediately. Once it's there, DO not touch it. Unless, of direction, it's for the aspect you are saving for.

2. positioned apart your lease In Increments

If you receive a commission monthly, positioned away from a lump sum in an account you don't touch (I placed mine in my savings, at the side of other financial savings, till lease day). If you receive a commission weekly or every 2nd week, put away a portion of your rent so that at the end of the month your lease cash will be magically sitting there and you might not blow one entire pay test on it.

3. Think about Spending In phrases of wants and needs

When you're spending cash, categorize what you are spending on as a need or a want. Food, bills, and rent are all wishes. A costly pair of event shoes is a want. Know the distinction, and prioritize the wishes. There will usually be greater wishes, however, your wishes are generally consistent. Easy, see?

4. Stick to One shape of fee

It is less complicated to tune what you are spending if you pay the use of one approach. Both go coins/debit or credit scores only, and it will be less complicated to the song you're spending. If you pick credit score, ensure you most effective spend what you can pay lower back! It turns into very obvious in no time if you're living out of doors your way.

5. Pay your bills As quickly As You Get Them

This must appear like a no-brainer but you'd be amazed by what you have to spell out now and then: pay your bills while they come! It's a whole lot much less formidable to pay the cost of one invoice than to discover your self-lumped with having to pay six right now. Do not allow them to pile up!

6. Set sensible goals

While you're budgeting, be real. Be sincere with yourself approximately what you may keep and what you can spend. Cash doesn't grow on timber, so constantly set desires which might be inside your means, and you will do simply satisfactory.

Chapter 4: Continued Financial Education

We go to law school to learn the laws of politics. School of Engineering is constructed to provide education about science and engineering. The art school teaches art, entertainment, and film-making. Business school talks about getting a good job after doing an MBA.

Finance school teaches you to be a financial expert and get employed in a good company. Take a look at the purpose of these schools. None of them talks about the real life skills.

Life requires you to be skillful with decision making. You must be cooperative. Learn to understand human relationships. It is extremely important to manage your financial situation.

Money is very important to live a good life. Poverty does not make you happy. It is a limitation that must be removed. Having said that, our educational system does not give any priority to financial education. Financial education is as important as learning to know your mathematics. In Mathematics, we are not taught to understand balance sheets. Most of us are simply ignorant on this topic.

Those of us who study financial accounting as a subject, cannot apply the information in personal life scenarios. I mean, you can learn to manage the finance of your company, but can you do the same for yourself? Living in debt is the American way. Our teenagers are paying credit card debt. Couples are in debt because they are starting a new life. Parents are bearing debt because of college fees. The debt equation has no solution. It does not have a quick fix.

You must learn some rules and the first one is to compromise. The second rule of financial education is to be creative. Think outside the box. There are a hundred ways to be a millionaire, but we never explore them. Do not worry growth follows knowledge. This book gives you the necessary knowledge and the motivation to follow what is written.

I am not sure about your financial education. About five years ago, I was in a debt of 12,000$. On top that, I was only earning 2,000$ monthly while my expenses were 3500$ per month. My debt was increasing, and my balance sheet was misbalanced. Managing that financial situation has given me the confidence to try out new ways. Financial education is not tough mathematics. It requires simple calculation like what are the possible paths to be a millionaire? With some calculation I found, that saving 5$ daily for 32 years results in one million dollars in your bank account.

The chances are that you can invest more than 5$, and you will be a multimillionaire in 32 years. If this calculation can make you a multi-millionaire, it can also pay your debt.

We need a clear understanding of our budget, expenses, and income. We must create our balance sheets. This segment will talk about it in detail.

Most people pay the cost of ignorance. It's not that they want to earn 50$. It is like they do not know how to earn 50,000$. The difference in earnings is the indication of lack of awareness. We stay in our comfort zone when we are not aware of opportunities. Maybe we can't see opportunities or we believe that the timing is not right us. Timing is never going to be perfect for you. Just like there is no right time to have a baby, there is no right time to take the next step. You must take action now.

You feel stuck in debt? There is a way to get out of this problem, but you must take action NOW! If you are earning 2000$ like me, you need to learn how to cut your expenses by 1500$. There are two concepts regarding this scenario. When faced with debt, people opt for two choices. Either they increase income to meet their life standard, or they simply reduce the living standard to match their earnings. Both of these are valid choices. You have the freedom to choice any option, but the selection reflects your mindset. It shows your thinking about money. Making money is a numbers game. There are no rules except the ones that emerge from real practice. Life has no rules. You have to design the rule and then, you must abide by these rules.

Coming to the money, most of us are unfamiliar with this numbers game. Money making is a mindset, you must learn it step by step. Let's take this debt as a learning opportunity. Let's master the art of money making and live a financially rich world.

Chapter 5: Why Budgeting Is Significant?

If you want to start a new behavior, you need good reasons to do so. Compelling reasons are proven to be very good for encouraging people and keeping them motivated. Without wasting any time, I will list the reasons why budgeting is essential.

Curb Overspending

Overspending happens when we spend our money without thinking about it. It also happens when we rely entirely on memory to keep track of our money. Memory is fallible, despite what you might believe about yours. Study after study shows that people overestimate how good their memory is. Relying on your mind to manage your finances leaves you open to vulnerabilities.

Overspending is a problem because it results in you having to borrow money from your future self. If you keep overspending, you will see yourself with less money to spend in the future because you have to cover your past debts. Overspending is among the most common and dangerous habits that many people have and spending wisely will help you avoid this. When you budget, you will find yourself with more money in your pocket and no need to overspend.

Budgeting helps by identifying where money is wasted, expenses you can cut, and funds to pay debts **(Bell, 2019)**.

Security

A lot of people assume that their jobs are secure because they have been working at a company for a long time, but unfortunately this is not true. Businesses face (random) challenges and their company can go under for various reasons, regardless of how big or small they are. A stark example is Lehman Brothers; it was founded in 1850, and business was good until it went under in 2008. I bet there were a few people who worked there who thought that would never happen. A budget helps cushion you for moments when your source of income disappears suddenly. While you figure out what to do next, you can tap into your savings.

Budgeting also provides security in other ways. For instance, if you happen to fall ill and your insurance won't cover all your expenses, you can use the money you saved instead of borrowing money.

Flexibility

People like to believe that they will always be the same people three years or five years from now. They think if they don't have kids now, they won't have them in five years. If they are content living in a small town, they will always feel that way. Or that, they will always want to work in the same industry doing the same thing for their entire life.

But as time goes, we change, the world changes, and we may want something different. A lot of the time, a big change like moving to another city, wanting to have kids, or learning new skills, requires money. Without money saved up, you won't be able to take advantage of opportunities that pop up. But having money saved up gives you the flexibility to act quickly without any hassles.

Emergencies

Budgeting can help you with emergencies. Emergencies happen suddenly, and they are often costly. An emergency can be anything. It can be your laptop getting stolen, your car breaking down, or you being diagnosed with a serious illness. Insurance and other financial products can help ease some of the pressure, but sometimes they are slow to act or will not help you. Always having money saved up protects you against that unpredictability.

Keeps You Focused

Life is more like a marathon, and long-term goals are important to make a life exciting and worth living. Having a budget helps us keep focused on our long-term goals and not be swayed by the present. In this way, it helps us achieve our long-term goals. A long-term goal can be buying a powerful computer so you can video edit or buying a new car. A budget makes saving easy and realistic. It reminds us of what our sacrifices are for, which ultimately keeps us motivated. Relying on your mind to sort out information is a difficult task; you will often lose sight of the bigger picture. With budgeting, you will stay focused.

Life-Changing Habits

In the beginning, budgeting will be difficult to put into place, but that will pass quickly. Transitioning your spending habits will not be a easy task because you have to adjust to a new system of doing things. Every now and again, you might falter, but it is the cumulative improvements and changes that will go a long way. Those new ways of doing things ripple into other parts of your life, making you a more focused, patient, and strategic individual. These ways of thinking and behaving will transform your life for the better. Your eyes will be open to how damaging certain habits are, and you won't want to go back.

Always Have Money for the Things You Need

Along with the many other benefits of budgeting your money, you will always have money for the things you need and the things that matter to you. You will never find yourself without things that are most important to you. For instance, if you find yourself running low on groceries and other essentials towards the end of the month, budgeting can help you stay supplied with enough groceries and essentials until your next paycheck, without having to borrow money or resort to credit cards to cover your expenses.

Chapter 6: Advantages Of Personal Finance Planning

Personal finance planning might be unnecessary for some people. Others just go with the flow and handle their finances day by day. They do not have a concrete and precise system on how they can maintain financial stability and security.

There are so many advantages to personal finance planning that a person can enjoy. A person just needs to put these steps into place to get the desired results about his finances.

Freedom to Indulge and Splurge

When you have personal finance planning and you are able to stick with your plans, you are more likely to have enough money saved up. Financial security lets you indulge on the things you like in life.

You do not have to borrow money from a friend or get a loan from the bank to travel or buy a new gadget. You can indulge in these things because you know that it would not break the bank.

Stay Out of Debts

Certain people can be compulsive buyers, buying stuff they see and like but do not need. This can hurt your finances especially when you give in to the urge knowing you do not have the money to buy it.

Your finances also suffer when you buy out of want knowing that you are saving money for other priorities. You can avoid this from happening to you through effective personal finance planning.

Planning means that you are already preparing for the future. You expect things to happen way before they do. By doing so, you make some precautionary measures like saving and investing.

When a person saves his money in a bank, it earns a small amount of interest every year. This is still good rather than just spending all your money. The best way to go is by investing.

When you invest your money, you can expect to get bigger and better outcome from your investment. Don't work for money, let money work for you. This will help you stay out and avoid debts.

Be Economically Safe

The economy is always shifting; inflation here and recession there happen all the time. That is why many people are scrimping up every penny they can save. They are aware that financial security is vulnerable.

Every generation appears to get lesser and lesser benefits. Time will come when even at an old age or during retirement, people would still work because they can no longer get their full pension. Planning your finances can help you secure your retirement and old age.

Get Better Outcome

When you do personal finance planning, you get better results. You can make your dreams come into reality because you know that the goals that you set are reachable and attainable.

You set realistic goals that you can achieve within a certain period. When you apply for a loan, you can pay it on time if you can plan on how you spend and save your hard-earned money.

Personal finance planning is important because with this, you can be successful in your finances. You can make better decisions when it comes to money and expenditures. You can buy things without fretting that it will hurt your budget and still stay out of debt that you cannot pay.

You will then be able to know how you are spending your money. Perhaps, money can make the world go round. Yet, with financial planning, it is you who control your own money that lets you control your world.

Chapter 7: Why Budgeting Is Important?

In normal routines, the budgeting is a modern way to help the funds reach the result of any activity. On the off chance that you've heard it once, you've heard it a thousand times: BUDGET YOUR MONEY! Monetary specialists and cash counselors have been yelling this mantra from the peaks for quite a long time.

This is only one of those money related exercises that can't be lectured enough. In the event that you and your family need monetary security, following a financial limit is the main answer.

Still not persuaded? The following are six valid justifications why everybody ought to make and adhere to a spending limit.

1. It Helps You Keep Your Eye on the Prize

A spending encourages you make sense of your long haul objectives and work towards them. In the event that you simply float erratically through life, hurling your cash at each entirely, gleaming article that happens to grab your attention, by what means will you ever set aside up enough cash to purchase a vehicle, take that outing to Aruba, or put an up front installment on a house?

A spending compels you to outline your objectives, set aside your cash, monitor your advancement, and make your fantasies a reality. Alright, so it might hurt when you understand that fresh out of the box new Xbox game or the ravishing cashmere sweater in the store window doesn't fit into your spending limit. In any case, when you advise yourself that you're setting something aside for another house, it will be a lot simpler to pivot and leave the store with next to nothing.

2. It Ensures You Don't Spend Money That You Don't Have

Excessively numerous shoppers go through cash they don't have—and we can owe everything to Mastercards. Indeed, the middle charge card obligation per family unit came to $2,300 in June 2019, as indicated by an ongoing report from ValuePenguin. Prior to the period of plastic, individuals would in general know whether they were living inside their methods. Toward the month's end, on the off chance that they had enough cash left to take care of the tabs and sock some away in reserve funds, they were on track. Nowadays, individuals who abuse and misuse charge cards don't generally acknowledge they're overspending until they're suffocating owing debtors.

Be that as it may, in the event that you make and adhere to a spending limit, you'll never end up in this unsafe position. You'll know precisely how a lot of cash you gain, the amount you can stand to go through every month and the amount you have to spare. Of course, doing the math and monitoring a financial limit isn't so a lot of fun as going on an improper shopping binge. Yet, take a gander at it along these lines: when your spend-cheerful companions are making a meeting with an obligation advocate this time one year from now, you'll be streaming off for that European experience you've been putting something aside for—or even better, moving into your new home.

3. It Leads to a Happy Retirement

Suppose you go through your cash capably, pursue your financial limit perfectly, and never convey Mastercard obligation. Bravo! Be that as it may, aren't you overlooking something? As significant all things considered to go through your cash shrewdly today, it's likewise basic to put something aside for your future.

A financial limit can assist you with doing only that. It's imperative to incorporate venture commitments with your financial limit. On the off chance that you put aside a part of your profit every month to add to your IRA, 401(k) or other retirement reserves, you'll in the end construct a pleasant savings. Despite the fact that you may need to forfeit a little now, it will be justified, despite all the trouble not far off. All things considered, okay rather spend your retirement hitting the fairway and taking excursions to the sea shore or filling in as a greeter at the nearby supermarket to make a decent living? Precisely.

4. It Helps You Prepare for Emergencies

Life is loaded up with sudden shocks, some superior to other people. At the point when you get laid off, become wiped out or harmed, experience a separation, or have a demise in the family, it can prompt some genuine money related strife. Obviously, it appears as though these crises consistently emerge even under the least favorable conditions conceivable time—when you're as of now stone cold broke. This is actually why everybody needs a rainy day account.

Your financial limit ought to incorporate a secret stash that comprises of at any rate three to a half year worth of everyday costs. This additional cash will guarantee that you don't winding into the profundities of obligation after an actual existence emergency. Obviously, it will set aside effort to set aside three to a half year of everyday costs.

Try not to attempt to dump most of your check into your just-in-case account immediately. Incorporate it with your financial limit, set sensible objectives and start little. Regardless of whether you put only $10 to $30 aside every week, your rainy day account will gradually develop.

5. It Sheds Light on Bad Spending Habits

Building a spending drives you to investigate your ways of managing money. You may see that you're burning through cash on things you needn't bother with. Do you genuinely observe every one of the 500 stations on your exorbitant broadened link plan? Do you truly require 30 sets of dark shoes? Planning enables you to reexamine your ways of managing money and re-center your budgetary objectives.

6. It's Better Than Counting Sheep

Following a spending will likewise assist you with grabbing increasingly shut-attention. How long have you thrashed around agonizing over how you were going to take care of the tabs? Individuals who lose rest over monetary issues are enabling their cash to control them. Reclaim the control. At the point when you spending plan your cash astutely, you'll never lose rest over budgetary issues again.

Advantages of Budgeting

Gives you authority over your cash — A financial limit is a method for being purposeful about the manner in which you go through and set aside your cash. It is said that with planning, you control your cash and not your cash controls you. Planning spares you the pressure of all of a sudden acclimating to absence of assets since you didn't at first arrangement how to spend them. It additionally causes you choose on the off chance that you need to forfeit transient spending like purchasing espresso ordinarily in return for a long haul advantage like a voyage excursion or another HDTV.

Keeps you concentrated on your cash objectives – You abstain from spending superfluously on things and administrations that don't add to accomplishing your monetary objectives. In the event that you are working with constrained assets, planning makes it simpler to make a decent living. Makes you mindful what is new with your cash – With planning, you are sure about what cash is coming in, how quick it goes out, and where it is going to. Planning spares you from pondering each month's end where your cash went. A financial limit empowers you to recognize what you can manage, make the most of purchasing and contributing chances, and plan how to bring down your obligation. It likewise mentions to you what is essential to you dependent on how you apportion your assets, how your cash is working for you, and how far you are towards arriving at your money related objectives.

Encourages you compose your spending and investment funds – By isolating your cash into classes of uses and reserve funds, a spending makes you mindful which classification of use takes which segment of your cash. That way, it is simple for you to make alterations. Spending limit likewise fills in as a source of perspective for arranging your bills, receipts, and budget summaries. At the point when the entirety of your monetary exchanges are composed for charge time or loan boss inquiries, you spare time and exertion.

Causes you to choose ahead of time how your cash will function for you.

Empowers you to put something aside for expected and unforeseen expenses – Budgeting enables you to plan to save cash for crisis costs.

Empowers you to speak with your huge others about cash – If you share your cash with your companion, family, or anybody, a spending limit can impart how you use cash as a gathering. This advances collaboration on working for basic monetary objectives and avoids strife on how cash is utilized. Making a financial limit pair with your life partner will dodge clashes and resolve individual contrasts on how your cash is spent. Planning trains relatives spending obligation and responsibility.

Gives you an early cautioning for potential issues – When you spending plan and take a "major picture" see, you will see potential cash issues ahead of time, and have the option to make changes before the issue shows up.

Encourages you decide whether you can take obligation and how much – Taking obligation isn't really a terrible thing if the obligation is essential or you can bear the cost of it. Planning gives you how much an obligation load you can practically take without being focused or if taking the obligation load is justified, despite all the trouble.

Empowers you to create additional cash – In planning, you get the opportunity to distinguish and kill superfluous spending like late charges, punishments and premiums. These apparently little sparing can include after some time.

Why Budgeting Is Important

Settling on solid budgetary choices is a significant piece of being monetarily secure. One of those choices is arranging your spending. Planning is an exceptionally simple and normal apparatus that can spare you hundreds if not a huge number of dollars over the long haul. Also you become progressively mindful of your ways of managing money and where your cash is going.

Reserve funds

You may believe that you have constantly on the planet to set aside cash, which is valid. However, it's never to soon to begin early. Taking care of cash into an investment account is critical for an effective money related future. Additionally it enables you to have a back-up plan on the off chance that you need additional cash or get low on money.

An investment funds is constantly a smart thought, and spares you stress and cerebral pains. Additionally by taking care of cash you will figure out how to live on spending plan and not spend more than you gain.

Back-Up Plan

Having a "Plan B" is constantly a smart thought. You can never be unreasonably arranged for what life has coming up and being monetarily secure is one approach to be prepared. Significant life changes can realize budgetary hardship, such as getting hitched or having an infant or a health related crisis and when these things occur, you need to be prepared.

Control Your Spending

Have you at any point been in a store and strolled in just requiring one thing however strolled pull out with three? Nearly everybody has done this yet planning can bend spending spills. At the point when you restrict yourself to a specific measure of cash for spending, you will effectively have the option to bend your propensities for purchasing additional things.

Plan Shopping Sprees

Because you spending plan your cash, doesn't mean you can't spend it. Some portion of planning will be making arrangements for enormous costs and binge spends is one of them. Because you are being keen with your cash doesn't mean you need to limit yourself from investing some of it.

By planning you will have the option to bear to spend some extra on specific things that you truly need without feeling regretful or terrible about it. Your arranging gives you space to take into account several costly things every so often without influencing your month to month costs adversely. You can spend and still take care of your tabs.

Not any more Late Payments

Being late on or to anything is rarely a decent sign. Being late on installments could make you fall into obligation and afterward make greater monetary issues for you. Planning will help you from missing installments or making late installments on significant bills since you will as of now have cash set aside for that bill. Your spending will ensure that each bill gets paid on time since it will be one of the top needs in your arrangement.

Accomplishing Your Goals

Defining objectives and contacting them, can be an exceptionally fulfilling procedure and fulfilling. Setting a reasonable and succinct spending plan will make them arrive at your objectives reliably and consistently. You will have the option to meet your objective of putting something aside for a vehicle or going on an extravagance excursion without inconvenience since you arranged. Likewise you will have the option to see your improvement and your exertion pay off.

Better Money Habits

Changing your ways of managing money can be a troublesome undertaking however planning can assist you with executing little changes that will go far. You will gradually begin to see changes in the manner you consider going through and how you go through your cash. You will start to see benefits and have the option to compensate yourself for having solid monetary practices. At last, you will have the option to spot terrible costs from great ones rapidly and be more able at sparing than spending.

Whenever you need to change your own monetary propensities, you must be happy to make an arrangement and set it into movement. An arrangement is nothing in the event that you don't actualize it into your life. By planning you will figure out how to settle on savvy spending choices while additionally sparing simultaneously.

Chapter 8: Money Is A Responsibility Not A Right

Being financially responsible is important no matter how old you are. If you have just gotten out of college or if you are middle-aged trying to correct past financial mistakes, you have to learn and apply the fundamentals of financial responsibility. To be financially responsible means that you live within your means and spend less than what you make.

Debts and Credit Cards If you really want to be responsible in the financial sense, you have to be aware of your debts and credit card payments. As much as possible, avoid getting a credit card and just use cash. However, if you cannot help it and you really need to own one, make sure that you are responsible with your payments. Do your best to pay off your balance in full every month. Remember that a credit card is not meant to make ends meet. Only get one so you can avoid carrying large amounts of cash around. One of the best perks of having a credit card is being able to earn reward points that you can use later on for rebates and other prizes. A credit card is also handy in case of emergencies. It is not wise to get a credit card for the sole purpose of paying off your debts or indulging in luxury items. You have to do the same with all other recurring payments with interest rates. When you pay interest on something, it means that you spend more for it than its purchase price; hence, you should think twice before you go for it. Yes, you may not be able to avoid paying interest on housing and car payments, but you can try to avoid paying interest on smaller things like appliances and electronic devices. Act in your Best Interest It's difficult for a lot of people to cut down on interest or borrow money. In practice, however, it all comes down to being able to tell the difference between luxuries and necessities. For instance, you may need a car, but it does not have to be an expensive model. Unless you can really afford to pay for it in cold, hard cash, then you should avoid getting one. Similarly, when choosing a house, go for one that you can afford. You may need a house, but it does not necessarily have to be a mansion. You have to be responsible in paying your mortgage. Ideally, your mortgage payments must not cost more than thirty percent of your monthly income. Do not get a house that costs more than twice or even five times your income per year. To avoid going overboard on your housing, you can make a down payment that is big enough to eliminate the need to pay for private mortgage insurance or PMI. If you cannot meet the guidelines for purchasing, you can opt to rent a house until you can afford to pay for one in full. Emergency Funds Being financially responsible also means that you are prepared for unexpected events. Ideally, you should have money set aside to live off for at least six months. In general, you can survive on your savings in case you got laid off your job or your business goes bankrupt.

Chapter 9: Classifying Your Expenses

Now that you were able to gather all the financial documents that will provide you with the necessary data, you are ready to sit down and start creating your budget. You can make use of a computer application to help you organize your data or you can go for the old school way by manually writing it down on a notebook or a ledger. Whichever method works for you, just be sure that the data is readily accessible and secure. You might want to consider creating a back-up file if you opt to use a computer software.

In creating a budget, there are two types of financial data that you need to be familiar with: your expenses and income. You may already have a basic idea of these two, but in this section of the book, they will be thoroughly discussed for you to carefully create your own budget.

The 2 Types of Expenses

Your expenses basically refer to the amount of money that you spend. It includes the money that you spend on groceries, clothes, fuel, utilities and the other wants and needs.

There are two kinds of expenses that you should be aware of. The first are the fixed expenses. These are the kind of expenses that do not vary each month and you have absolutely no control over their price. Examples of fixed expenses include house rent, car mortgage, insurance fees and loan payments.

The second kind is your variable expenses. These are the kind of expenses which you have control over. Their amount depends entirely on your discretion or consumption. Examples of variable expenses include utilities and groceries. The more food that you consume, the higher your expense on groceries and restaurant bills will be. Likewise, the more electronic appliances that you have in your home, the higher your electrical bill will be.

Take out all the receipts that you have previously gathered and scan through them. You will now sort these bills and receipts into two: your fixed and variable expenses. Put your receipts of fixed expenses in one file and receipts of your variable expenses in another. Next, list them all in your record book. First, write down the label "FIXED EXPENSES" and list all your fixed expenses incurred. Add it all up and encode the total amount. Next, write down the label "VARIABLE EXPENSES" and list all your variable expenses made. Follow the same process. Add it all up and put in the total amount. Finally, add your total fixed expenses and variable expenses then label it as "TOTAL EXPENSES." It should look like this:

EXPENSES FOR THE MONTH OF _____

FIXED EXPENSES

1. House mortgage $2,500

2. Car loan $1,000

3. Bank loan $800

Total   Fixed $4,300
Expenses

VARIABLE
EXPENSES

1. Groceries $550

2. Electricity $430

3. Water $260

4. Fuel $390

Total   Variable $1,630
Expenses

TOTAL EXPENSES   **$5,930**

Do not make any adjustments yet. Just record your data as it is and be sure to double check your receipts and calculations before proceeding to the next step. You need to be careful as one mistake can already affect the rest of the budget you are creating.

Chapter 10: Creating A Basic Budget Step-By-Step

You know the importance of a budget and what methods are out there. Maybe there's one that stands out and you know that's the style you'll choose. Maybe you aren't sure and are going to try a couple to see what sticks. No matter what you choose, there are certain steps you'll need to take and information to gather. This chapter walks you through the process. By the end, you'll have a budget and a clear idea of your overall net worth.

Determining your net worth

Before you start your budget, it's a good idea to figure out your net worth first. Your net worth is essentially a measure of your financial situation and health. It will help inform your budget, especially when it comes to how much money you put towards savings and debt. You get your net worth by adding up all of your assets (which includes a car, savings accounts, a 401(k), any investments, etc) and then subtracting your debts. If you own a home, home equity also factors into your net worth. What is home equity? It's the part of your home that you actually own, and it increases over time if the property value goes up and as you pay down your mortgage. You can determine your equity by starting with your home's value and subtracting what you owe on the mortgage or in home loans.

Let's look at an example of a person's net worth:

Assets and debt

Chris is 25-years old and recently graduated college. She owes $40,000 in student loans. She does have a job, but since she just started, she only has $1,500 in her 401(k). For savings, she has $1,000. She rents an apartment, so she doesn't have a mortgage, and her car is worth around $10,000. She still owes $8,000 on it, however. She also does not have any credit card debt.

What are her assets? Her car ($10,000), her 401(k) ($1,500) and her savings account ($1,000). That means she has a total of $12,500 in assets. For her debts, she has that auto loan of $8,000 and student loans of $40,000. That totals $48,000. Subtract that number from assets, and you end up with -$35,500.

What does a negative net worth mean?

When you subtract your debt from your assets, it isn't unusual to get a negative number, because your debts exceed your assets. This is especially common for someone young like Chris. It also happens if you have financial struggles like credit card debt, significant medical debt, or are not working a job that's able to meet your lifestyle needs. How does someone like Chris with a negative net worth improve her situation? The more debts Chris pays off and more assets she can accumulate, the better her net worth will be. It can be a slow process, but as long as that debt number is getting smaller, she's on the right track.

Creating Chris' budget

When Chris creates a budget, she wants to focus on paying off those student loans while continuing to contribute to her savings and 401(k). However, she still has monthly expenses she needs to pay, too. With all that in mind, let's create a budget for her.

Step 1: Figure out your total monthly income

How much money does Chris make? She has a salaried job, so finding out her monthly income isn't difficult. If she had an hourly job, however, it could be trickier. To get the best idea, she would look at the past 6-12 months and average it out. In addition to her day job, Chris also does freelancing work online, which adds about $300 per month to her income.

When determining your monthly income, record everything you make.

Step 2: Figure out your monthly expenses

We know that Chris is paying student loans and the loan on her car, so a portion of her income always goes towards those every month. She also has to pay rent and electricity (the other utilities are included in her rent), internet, cable, groceries, entertainment, gas, and so on. She collects all this information and adds it up. Those variable expenses (which we talked about earlier and include anything that changes month to month, like entertainment) are a bit trickier to calculate, so she just guesses for now.

Step 3: Set goals

Chris now has all the information she needs for her budget, so it's time to choose a budget style. First, she thinks about her financial goals. She's okay with living in an apartment for a while, so house ownership isn't a priority. However, she really wants to get rid of those student loans as soon as possible, especially considering the high interest rates. She wants to increase the amount she's paying on them every month, so she decides to go with a 50/10/40 budget. She commits to setting aside a big chunk of her income towards those loans, and keeping her "wants" expenses really lean. Since she's most concerned with the loans, she decides that most of the money for that category will go towards loans, with just 10% towards savings, so the budget actually breaks down like this:

50% towards needs

10% towards entertainment

30% towards student loans

10% towards savings

Consider your own financial goals when selecting a budget style. Chris doesn't have credit card debt, but if that's something that's an issue for you, maybe a cash-only budgeting style will help you from racking up more. Maybe you really want a house in the next few years, so you go with the pay-yourself-first method to keep building up those savings. All the budgeting styles could work for a variety of scenarios and goals; it's really up to you and what you like best. Regardless of the style you choose, always keep the big picture at the back of your mind.

Step 4: Make adjustments

Now with a budget style and goals set, Chris can start following a budget. She breaks down the 50/10/40 into actual dollars. As time goes on, she pays attention to where she's overspending (she has a fondness for video games) and makes adjustments to her lifestyle to fit into her budget. When Christmas gets closer, she adjusts her budget again to accomodate a plane ticket back to her hometown. That means switching her normal Starbucks in the morning for the office brew, resisting going out to eat for the next three months, and picking up more weekend freelance work. Reviewing and adjusting your budget is a consistent step that keeps you on track and in control.

Chapter 11: How To Maintain A Successful Budget Plan

If you are the head of household, you should always be aware of how much your family spends and many times you may find yourself creating a budget on paper, which is the easy part. Sticking to your budget is a definite challenge! It's great to have a budget written down, but until you put it to action, it is only words on paper. You must make a willing effort to follow your planned budget. You can have and maintain a successful budget when you follow these five simple steps to stay on target.

Budget Commitment

Without a commitment to put your budget plan into action, then all you are doing is just writing words on paper that will soon be tossed into the trash. Make it a daily habit of reviewing your expenses and income so there is always an understanding of where your finances stand, which serves as a consistent reminder to stick to your goals.

Lifestyle Changes

Simple changes in your lifestyle can make it a lot easier to stay within your budget. Packing a lunch for work or school can save you to five to seven dollars a day on average. Multiply that by five to six days and that is twenty five to thirty five dollars a week. Multiply that by four weeks and that's $100 to $140 a month! Now you see how quickly it adds up.

Make it a point to prepare yourself on a weekly basis before going to the supermarket. Start by planning your weekly meals and creating a shopping list that will be just what you need to make your meals. Take advantage of days when a store is offering additional in-store savings. When you shop with a list, you are less likely to overspend and stay within your planned and targeted budget.

Keep Your Focus on the End Goal

When you created your budget, you probably had an end goal in mind. Whether that goal was financial freedom, saving for a dream vacation, the purchase of a new home, or simply getting out of living pay check to pay check. Write your initial goal on the top of your monthly budget as a daily reminder and motivator that you are doing all this to reach your end goal.

Think Before You Spend

When you go shopping, venturing into a mall or store filled with the latest gadgets or new clothing trends will remind you of your end goal. Ask yourself: "Is this something that will help or hinder me from reaching my budget's end goal. In other words, is it something I need or want?" Learning to identify the difference between wants and needs is a huge step in accomplishing your end goal.

Pay Cash Not Credit

When you go shopping, keep your credit cards at home. The amount that you pay in interest will rob you of your savings toward your end goal. Credit cards tend to give you a false sense of wealth when used outside of your purpose budget. If you don't have the cash, then it's probably something not worth buying. Remember, your desire is to stay on target with your budget and this will reward you in the long run.

A budget is meant to give you the liberty to accomplish your real desires and keep you free from the chains of debt that hold so many. Your desire to keep a budget is meant to make your life more enjoyable especially when you stay within your guidelines.

Sticking with a budget commitment where you are willing to have lifestyle changes, keeps you thinking before you spend and paying with cash not credit, will have well on your way to establishing and maintaining a successful budget.

Chapter 12: Debt Management Strategies

Do this: obtain a grand total of all the income you've earned since you got your mortgage loan. Once done, deduct your total income from the total value of the loan. How much difference did you get? If you obtained a positive number, you know that if you've been wiser, your mortgage would have already been paid. But that's far from reality because no matter how much money you make, you still need to live.

The situation above merits the need to have a proactive way when it comes to dealing with debt: responsible management. The management aspect does not only cover repayment. It also covers saving for additional payment. This is where the concept of budgeting comes in, too. But before we start, let's get you to analyze a few things first.

Income and Debt Analysis

First, you have to have a clear idea of where your income is coming from. You also need to know how much you're making exactly. Hence, you need to make a list. Second, think about how much money you're currently making from all of your sources. List all of these sources alongside the amount you're getting. Obtain your monthly total income. Make sure that you only add your net income and not your gross income.

Third, list all of the outstanding debts you have. Include the outstanding amount plus the interest rate you're paying for each month. Obtain a total. Afterwards, calculate your Debt-to-Income Ratio.

Debt-to-Income Ratio Calculation

When calculating your debt-to-income ratio, you need two elements: your recurring monthly debt and your gross monthly income. Since it's a ratio you're trying to obtain, you need to express your calculation in percentage form. Here is an example:

Recurring monthly debt - $1000

Gross monthly income - $2000

Debt-to-income ratio – 50%

The formula is [1000/2000] x 100 = 50%

Ideally, the ratio you'll obtain should not exceed 20%. If it does, you have every reason to be concerned. Getting something lower than 20% is not something you should take comfort on either. While getting 0% only happens when you do not have any debts, the lower the ratio you get the better.

Expense Analysis

Finally, after analyzing your income and your debts, and after obtaining your debt-to-income ratio, you need to assess your expenses. To help you out, you can retrieve your transaction records online. What have you been spending money on? Are these expenses something that you really need or something that you only want? Which of these expenses can you cut back on? Which of these expenses can you cut off for good?

The rationale behind cutting off and cutting back on your expenses is the chance of you increasing the amount of money you can save to either go to your savings account or to be applied on an outstanding debt. Once you review you expense activity and have come up with a budget, it's time to decide on how you can repay your outstanding debts.

Debt Repayment Strategies

There are a lot of debt repayment strategies out there, but only two has so far proven to offer the best results: the Snowball Method and the Avalanche Method.

The Snowball Method

The Snowball Method involves paying smaller debts first before taking care of the bigger one. Remember the list you created when you analyzed your income and debts? You can go back to it now and check which of your loans have the highest principal balance and interest rate.

The advantage of using the Snowball Method is that you take active control in debt repayment. Since you're taking care of smaller debts, there's a great chance of your being able to progress through payment in a rather shorter amount of time. Then again, the downside is that because you're not dealing with the bigger debt right away, you still need to pay a high amount for it monthly.

The Avalanche Method

The Avalanche Method involves paying the bigger debts first before taking care of the smaller ones. You can also refer to the same list containing your income and debts to determine which method is suitable for you. You can even make your calculations to see which of the methods offers you more savings.

The advantage of the Avalanche Method obviously lies in the elimination of the most burdensome debt. However, because it's a debt with the highest amount or interest rate, it might take longer for you to repay it. If that happens, you'd have to put up with multiple payments required from your smaller loans.

There you have it. The direction you prefer to take when it comes to managing your debts is entirely up to you. If you can't decide, there's always that option of talking to a credit management professional. That way, you can also go through other options when it comes to debt management.

Now that you know how you can potentially get out of debt for good, it is time that you polish your financial goals. If things will work out the way you planned them to, you have a good chance of achieving the financial goals that you set in the next chapter.

Chapter 13: Creating A Financial Plan

Creating a financial plan for your household is an absolute necessity. When you have a household budget, you can manage money effectively so that you and your family will never have to worry about not having enough money for food, utilities, emergencies, medicine, and so on. Without a budget plan for your household though, you are actually putting your family at risk. If you want to avoid those unpleasant situations where you've run out of money for something important, create your budget plan today. To begin, it is crucial that you set your financial goals. The main point of having a budget is to attain these goals. They must be categorized into two sections: long-term and short-term goals. When you have a goal in mind, you will find it easier to follow your budget. Long-term financial goals may include retirement plans and saving up for a new car or a house, while short-term financial goals can include eliminating your credit card debt, paying monthly bills on time, etc. Separate all your expenses into two categories: bare necessities and optional expenses. The bare necessities are the ones you need in order to survive (ex: grocery shopping), and the optional expenses are the things you want but can live without (ex: weekly pedicures). Bare necessities can also be defined as 'priorities' while the optional expenses can be described as 'luxuries'.

Now, make a list of all your bare necessities. Keep in mind; these are the things that you absolutely must spend money on and won't be able to live without. Items in this list should include Food, Rent or Mortgage, Utilities, etc. Although these are mentioned as the items that you need in order to survive, it's really up to you to include in the list the items that you personally categorize as 'needs' and to remove items that you don't consider a necessity. If diapers and infant formula are among your household expenses at the moment, then don't forget to include these in your list of necessities. Your children's tuition fees can also make this list. However, when creating the budget for your family's basic needs, further classify whether these needs are monthly, quarterly, semi-annually, or yearly. That way you can allot funds effectively. It is important that you make your list as detailed and as accurate as possible so that you can create an effective budget plan. Add up all your expenses for the basics and you'll get an idea of how much money you need monthly. There's no need to agonize if most of your income goes on the bare necessities. Remember the rule. Decrease your expenses or increase your income. Now that you are aware that most of your income just goes on your family's basic needs, it may be time to find cheaper alternatives or to consider other income streams. Perhaps you need to start looking for a better paying job, get a second job, or consider a sideline for additional income. Needless to say, allot money for the items on this list and don't 'borrow' this amount for other kinds of expenses. Always stick to your budget.

All other expenses that didn't make your 'Bare Necessities' list will go on your 'Optional Expenses' list. Items in this list will include Travel, Hobbies, Shopping, and many more. However, if there is no leftover from your income after allotting for the basics, then you cannot create a budget for the items in this category. Savings, Investment Money, Emergency Fund and Retirement Fund are not really classified as expenses. Just like optional expenses, you can only allot money for these if there is a leftover in the income. Unless you placed Savings or an Emergency Fund under Bare Necessities, you can include these in creating your budget. If you have some extra money left after the basics have been removed, assign an amount for these and stick to it. For example, allot $500 per month for Spending Money which you can use for all your personal needs. As for your Savings,

Emergency Fund, and Retirement Fund, it would be best to open separate bank accounts for each and just deposit monthly the amount you allot.

By now, you're aware of the importance of clearly defining your expenses and the other things you want to allot money for. That will help you in creating a good monthly budget for your household.

Chapter 14: Budgeting For Financial Freedom

To build wealth, you need to learn how to create a personal budget. A budget helps you learn how to cut back on your expenses, use your financial resources judiciously and get out of debt faster.

Without a budget, you tend to spend on your needs and wants whether you can afford them or not. Most people who are neck deep in credit card debt today find themselves in that situation because of a lack of a working budget.

If you truly desire financial freedom, you need to learn how to create a budget and stick with it. Here are a few tips to help guide you:

Check Your Account Balance: Look into your bank accounts (checking and savings account) as well as any other investment accounts or financial instruments you have. This will help you determine your net worth.

Determine Your Average Monthly Income: How much do you earn a month of average? You should be able to make a prediction based on your past income history.

Determine How Much You Owe: Do you have any debts that you are currently servicing i.e. car loans, student loans, credit card debts, mortgages and any other debts? Determine how much this takes from you every month.

Determine Your Net Worth: This is really simple. Just deduct the total debts you owe from the assets and money you have. If you discover that you have a negative or low financial net worth (your outstanding debts exceed or equal the value of assets and cash that you have), that's a red flag. It shows that you haven't been doing too well with your financial management and financial freedom is still far away. You have to work hard to reverse this situation.

In the next few chapters, we will discuss how to pay off your debts faster.

Determine Your Monthly Expenses: Your expenses can be classified into two categories; recurring and non-recurring expenditure. Your recurring expenditure includes things like utility bills and other regular bills that you have to deal with every month.

The non-recurring expenses are expenses that don't come monthly but once in a while like school fees, buying of appliances and so on.

Create Your Budget: There are two ways to create a personal budget. You can either used fixed sums or percentages although using percentages is better as it helps you adjust to your reality.

Dave Ramsey, a financial guru set down some guidelines that you can use to create your own personal budget.

Category	Percentage of Overall Income
Housing	25-35%
Utilities	5-10%
Transportation	10-15%
Healthcare	5-10%
Food	5-15%
Investments/Savings	10%
Debt Payments	5-10%
Charitable Giving	5-15%
Entertainment/Recreation	5-10%
Misc Personal	2-7%

This is just a guideline as no two people have the same needs and financial circumstances. It is therefore up to you to customize your budget to suit your personal circumstances but always remember to set aside the very important 10% savings, as it would serve as your foundation for wealth generation.

The Envelop System

As far as money management and real life budgeting goes, nothing beats the classic envelop system. In this method, you simply take an envelope for every expense item that you intend to incur during a certain period (say a month) then put in whatever money you believe would be sufficient (base this on your spending history). Ensure that you've already set aside your savings when doing this to eliminate the likelihood of you going after the savings. Pick money from the relevant envelope whenever you want to incur any expenditure. For example, if you want to incur money on transport and groceries, pick money from different envelops (transport and groceries respectively). Any change that remains will have to be divided properly across the different envelopes. This method helps you to realize that you don't have money for items that you've not budgeted for. And if you run out of money on one envelop, you shouldn't just pick money from other envelops and expect that you won't experience financial difficulty in that period; you will have to sacrifice something if you don't want that to happen. It is very easy to know which areas of your life tend to have many 'emergencies' because even after putting money in the envelope, you may find yourself picking money from some envelopes.

Note: Don't have the habit of picking money from one envelop when you've run out of money in another envelop. Unless it is something you cannot live without (e.g. transport money or groceries money), anything else can wait until your next reimbursement. For instance, if you've run out of money in your 'clothes' envelope, you have to wait for the next period.

Tip: You don't have to use a physical envelop for this. Some of the modern online applications have this feature.

Some of these include Mint.com and Mvelops.com.

Note: No budgeting system will magically transform your life. You MUST have the will and the desire to make it work; the nature of the system will simply facilitate you to make this possible.

To expound on this, let's move on to discussing savings.

Chapter 15: Why You Should Save

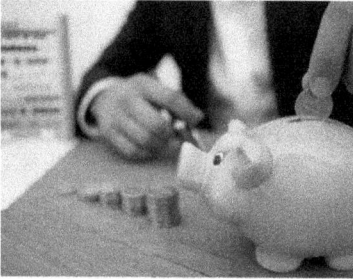

Before you decide to save, you need to set your reason why you save. The big goal may be to become a millionaire. It's a good goal because it will motivate you to save even more if you already have hundreds of thousands in your account. However, you should also have smaller goals so that you can see rapid progress and stay motivated.

Find your **WHYs!**

You may want to do further education which you have to pay for yourself, you might want to have a certain amount on your account before you start a family, you finally want to fly to Japan or South America, or you would like to buy a car or house. Whatever your small and intermediate goals are, write them down. Also, write down the number you want to see in your account when you want to fulfill the goals.

If you're at 0 at the moment and would like to receive a pay advance every month, it's not realistic that you will be at 200'000 in a year. But 20'000 to 40'000 are possible if you stick to the savings tips from this book.

Create a vision board

If you're a visual person, you can design a small vision board with your savings goals.

You cut out pictures of the desired items (e.g. car, pictures of beautiful beaches) or you draw something yourself and write down your desired fortune as a number. This way you can see your goal every day and you will be constantly guided by it.

Surely you have already thought about which savings goal you would like to achieve. Quickly look at the next chapter before you design your vision board to pick a realistic number. Of course, you may set your goal a bit higher, but the feeling of success will be much better if you set yourself a realistic goal and then see that your wealth is actually growing.

Chapter 16: Spending Habits To Save Money

If you're anything like me, you probably are in impulse shopper. The trouble with this is that we often buy things we really don't need just because we like the way that they look. It's okay to treat yourself at times, but when you find that you spend more on junk than necessity, you really do have a problem. This is just one of the negative spending habits that people struggle with. If we could focus on saving rather than spending, we could greatly increase our wealth. Let's take a look at some ways that we can change some of our negative spending habits!

Use coupons

Believe it or not, you don't have to be an extreme couponer in order to use coupons to save money. Manufacturers put out coupons to encourage you to buy their items. Use that to you benefit. Just make sure that when you are looking for coupons that you only clip the ones that you really need and not just because the coupon looks good. It's easy to spend unnecessary money with coupons if you're not careful.

Buy with cash

If you budget with cash and only spend cash, you won't be tempted to use credit cards to make your purchases. Cash can take the place of even your debit cards. Once you spend all of the cash, you're done and need to wait until the next round of budgeted cash comes around.

Go generic when possible

Many named brand items have generic equivalents that work just as well, if not better than the originals. Try buying generic whenever you can. You can typically save one to two dollars an item by doing this. Just think about how much you can really save on your grocery cart using this method!

Buy only what is needed

People love to buy the extras simply because they look good on the shelf. However, many of these items are totally unnecessary and just add extra expenses to your budget. Really think about whether or not you need the extra before purchasing it. You might be thankful that you did!

Stock up when things go on sale

If something that you use on a regular basis goes on sale, don't be afraid to stock up on it when it's on sale. Just be careful if it is something that can go bad easily. You don't want to stock up on items that will ultimately go to waste because they are past their expiration dates. By stocking up on what you use when it's discounted, you can ultimately save a nice amount of money!

Learn to bargain shop

For items that you don't buy all the time, try buying off of the clearance rack or the sale shelves. This works great with clothing. You can get some great prices on clothing by looking at the sales and the sale racks. Also, if you're not totally opposed to it, shopping in thrift stores can help you find great bargains and save you money.

Avoid higher priced stores

There are always stores that sell similar items. Some will charge more for the same thing. Most of us know which stores have the reputation for doing this. It might be a good idea to totally avoid these stores and only shop at them when you know that they are offering a good sale. By doing this, you are avoiding be trapped into paying more for what you can get elsewhere for less.

Changing the way we shop can be one great way in changing our monetary flow. The money we save can be used elsewhere or even put into a savings account to save for our futures. Try cutting back where you can see if you can see a real difference in your monthly expenses!

Chapter 17: What Is Budgeting And Why Is It So Important?

Budgeting is the process of creating a system and process on how to spend and save your money. This system and process is called a **budget.** Creating a system allows you to determine in advance (if you stick with it) whether you will have enough money to do the things you need or want to do.

Budgeting also is the act of balancing your income with your debts and expenses. If your expenses outweigh the income coming in, then you have a major cash flow problem and you will end up sinking further and further into debt and will struggle getting out of it. If this is you, I'm glad you picked up this book.

Most people don't even realize they are spending more than what they are earning and are sinking into a financial hole they will have a hard time getting out of it.

Why is Budgeting So Important?

Since having a budget allows you to create a spending process for your money, if you stick with it, it will help ensure that you will hopefully always have enough money for the things that you need first, want second such as the things that you deem important to you.

Following a budget or spending plan will also help you get out of debt or at the very least help you get you into a process where you will eventually get out of debt.

Budget Projections, Planning and Forecasting

Once you create your initial budget and begin to use it, you will get a good feel for how it can help you keep your finances on track. Once you get used to this system, you will then want to map out your spending for the next 6 months to a year down the road.

By doing this, you can easily predict what your finances will be like and whether you will have extra money down the road. You can then identify ways to get out of the problematic time periods and keep your finances balanced and manageable.

Projecting your budget out into the future allows you also to forecast how much money you will be able to save for any personal goals such as buying a home, new vehicle or even going on vacation.

Creating a budget is typically created using a spreadsheet and it provides an organized and easy way of understanding of how much money you have coming in and how much money you are getting rid of. Creating this spreadsheet is an invaluable tool to help you prioritize your choices and your money no matter how much or little you may have financially.

Planning and monitoring your budget will also help you identify where your money is being wasted and how to make changes quickly before problems arise. When you start to see a breakdown of your income, expenses and spending habits you will be surprised what you find and how quickly spending will add up.

Simply put, a budget is an itemized summary of likely income and expenses for a given period. It helps you determine whether you can grab that bite to eat or should head home for a bowl of soup. It is typically created using a spreadsheet, and it provides a concrete, organized, and easily understood breakdown of how much money you have coming in and how much you are letting go. It's an invaluable tool to help you prioritize your spending and manage your money—no matter how much or how little you have.

Creating a budget will help decrease your stress levels because with it, there are no surprises and you can make better financial decisions.

Chapter 18: Finances, From 30,000 Feet

Now that you've sorted out what you've made and spent, you can now fill out a spreadsheet so that you can track your expenses.

Please click on this link to access the spreadsheet, and I will guide you through on how to fill it out: First, press the 'ctrl' (or 'command' on a Mac) key on your keyboard, and then click this link: http://ow.ly/Zkm3V (Or just copy and paste it into your browser!)

Note: you'll need to log into a Google account and save a copy of the spreadsheet to use it.

Note that the spreadsheet has twelve monthly tabs. Within each tab is a column for each day of the month. Please remember that if you are married, it is highly recommended that you make this a "household" budget, and you should include your spouse's information.

Income

In the first line, "Salary", input the total income that you make from your regular job, or line of work. If you have a pay slip, look at the actual take home amount or the amount that was deposited into your account, and record this **net** amount that you took home for the month. "Salary" in this sense, also refers to other forms of compensation, such as commissions and bonuses, and aren't limited to fixed monthly compensation received.

In the next line, "Misc", input any money that you received from different sources not related to regular income received from your work. The most common items are interest received on savings accounts, and income tax refunds. This may also include gifts or bequests.

Expenses

The categories in these line items are generally self-explanatory. The following areas may require a little extra attention.

136

Under "Utilities", you may have other fixed monthly expenses, such as water, gardening, pest control, and pool maintenance. Decide if you want to record these items under "Electric", or "Gas". The requirement is that you need to be consistent on a month-to-month basis on where you will want to include these items to make each item comparable on a month-to-month basis.

The next item, "Household" expenses will most probably include your biggest line items, so pay extra attention to them. If you pay a mortgage for the place that you live in, input the mortgage payment in the "Rent" line item. Any other expenses that may be separately billed such as renter's or homeowners' insurance should be included under "Rent." Be careful that you don't "double count" items already included in your mortgage bill, such as homeowner's insurance.

The line item, "Groceries", should include the consumable items that you regularly purchase for your day-to-day needs. This is not just limited to food, but also to items such toiletries and cleaning supplies. The general rule of thumb is that if it came from your shopping cart then they are groceries. To simplify matters, take the supermarket or grocery receipt total, and record this on the spreadsheet directly. Under "Furnishings", input items such as furniture, and relatively large expenses such as drapes, and decorative items, such as painting and carpets. Also include bigger-ticket electronic items such as computer equipment, such as desktops, laptops, and printers.

Expenses directly paid to a hospital or clinic where you don't expect reimbursement you can place in the "Doctor" line item in the "Health" category. This also applies to any deductibles that you will pay and any uncovered tests or treatment that you may need to pay for.

Depending on your spending habits, "Lifestyle" may be a big expense category. Cruises, vacation packages, and road trips should be under "Entertainment". You should include items such as movies and shows for this line item. Gambling, attending sporting events, and bowling nights, should also be included in the "Entertainment" line item.

Under "Travel and transport", include any other vehicle maintenance expenses such as oil changes, tune-ups, or repairs. In most cases, do not record any expenses if these are office-related, and you expect reimbursement for them. If you incur any transportation expenses related to vacations or getaways, include these as under the "misc" line item in the "Treats" category. If you are paying off a car loan, decide where you want to put it in this category. Just remember to be consistent from month to month.

Under the "Treats" category, the "Eating out/takeaway" line should include things like a night out with friends and family (or a big night out drinking!).

If you have monthly expenditures related to paying down a credit card or an existing loan, decide on where you want to put this on a spreadsheet. The best way is to determine where the original credit charges and loan proceeds went to, and record the payment in the appropriate category. For example, if you mostly used your credit card to finance living room furniture, include the credit card payment under "Furnishings."

After you have done a good job figuring out your budget, you don't want to just walk away from the spreadsheet and forget about it. You need to have it printed out or have it downloaded on a portable device and make it available all the time to remind (and even warn!) yourself of your new spending patterns, and any limits or restrictions that you may need to place on yourself and your wallet.

Now you actually have to control your spending.

Chapter 19: Easy Bargain Shopping Tips Guaranteed To Save You Money

Here are some of the bargain shopping tips I use to save money

Boldness pays

Often times, consumers are shy. I cannot tell you how many times I have bought an item at asking price on one day only to go back to the same store a few days later and find the items is on sale. If you see an item you like, you should make sure to ask if you can get a discounted price. This is especially true for clothing stores.

Social-stalk your favorite store

I do not mean that you go all social pervert on your favorite store; I simply mean follow them on Twitter and like their Facebook page. Why is this important in bargain hunting? With the advent of social media, most major retail stores have also "gone-social". This means that even before they display the discount banner on their glass doors, or place an ad in the paper or billboard, they announce the discounts to their social community first. Following this trick will make sure you are always among the first to know and to get to the store before other shoppers snatch up the real bargains; the real value for money items.

Free shipping is your friend

One of the major downsides of online shopping is the shipping cost. Often times, I have found many discounted items only to proceed to checkout and realize that the shipping cost plus the buying price is way above what I would pay had I bought the items off a shelf. Even though we shall look at online bargain shopping in depth, I would suggest you go for deals that offer free shipping or buy from stores such as Talbots and J crew that offer free shipping on online and catalog items.

Be mindful of the sale tax amount

Some of the ways you can use to avoid the sale tax is to buy from an online out-of-state store and ship the merchandise. Additionally, most states offer discount sale tax on their website. Therefore, you should visit your State website to see which item you can discount (sale tax discount). A good case and point is the fact that most States do not tax clothing purchases under $100. This gives you the option of breaking down your large purchase into smaller below $100 consignments.

Dear Old compare cliché

This will come up repeatedly throughout our bargain hunting lessons. There is no way you can learn if you are really getting a bargain without comparing prices and merchandise in other stores. However, comparison from store to store may be hectic, and because we live in an already hectic world, you may lack the time to "store hop" while comparing; thus, online searches may be the best option. Most major retailers across the U.S and UK have a website. Visit favorite store website and when you snag an item, visit its competitors' website to see which price they have on the same or similar item. More often than not, you will find that this will always save you some money. Additionally, you can use sites such as shopstyle.com to compare store prices.

Chapter 20: Establish The Goals You Want To Accomplish

What is to establish the goal you want to accomplish?

Establishing the goals you want to accomplish is very simple. For your convenience, I have provided a worksheet called, "**My Goals Worksheet**", which is included with this e-book and should be used in conjunction with this section of the book.

The main aspect of this is to write down your goals, your bucket list, or anything you want to accomplish in your life. You may already have these things in mind, but do you have a plan to achieve them? If you don't, it is time to write them down.

How to Establish The Goals You Want To Accomplish

I want you to remember every single aspect of the dream(s) you may have had years ago, before thinking they would never happen. Write them down in the worksheet. Anything you can think of that might seem crazy, write those goals down too. **Anything is achievable!**

Now that you wrote down your goals; you now need a plan. Open the **Saving Goals Worksheet** for this part. There's 2 type of goals. The short-term goals and the long term goals. Short-term goals are things you want to accomplish in the **next 1-4 months** and long-term goals for the **next 5-12 months**. If you want to realize a goal in 4 months, odds are that you need to start saving now; or should I say yesterday! Follow these steps to fill out the worksheet:

Write down each of your goals in a chronological order, from top to bottom

Determine the amount of money you want to save per month for each goal

Make sure that the amount you plan on saving is available, according to your Funds

Available section in the Monthly Income & Expenses Worksheet

When is it necessary?

If you're an individual looking to get the most out of his life, do it the sooner possible. You will feel happy knowing that after each day you are reaching something. Achieving goals makes you feel proud and you will be less likely to quit them. **Set goals, build plan and achieve them.**

Anything you want to afford, you can. If you can't afford it with months of savings, it might be a good solution to update your knowledgebase as it relates to increasing your income and saving the extra money you're making.

What does it mean to entrepreneurs?

In business, you need to know your goals from the very beginning. In fact, our goals are what push us to build businesses in the first place, so make sure you have them written down along with a strong plan.

Example: If you're looking to build a 6 figure income business, you might need the capital to increase your productivity or talent and one day reach the 6 figure income. There's a way to do it with low capital, but you need to figure that out. A plan is the best way to make sure it happens since you write down the steps to get there. It's pretty much the same as visiting a city you've never been to without a map or navigation. You will get lost!

As an entrepreneur, establishing your goals will not only give you a clear idea of what to accomplish and how, but it will also help you. Your daily tasks should come before reaching your goals. As I mentioned before, writing down your goals increases the odds of you realizing them. You want a successful business, right?

Chapter 21: How To Be Financially Savvy

Knowledge dear women, will form your foundation to be the perfect manager of your finances. Being a traditional homemaker with zero knowledge of money matters, will only make things harder for you and your growth will be stagnated. We are not aiming to be underdogs of the situation here. Most regular housewives only take charge of the monthly expenses handed over to them by their spouses. They do not take interest in how the money inflow is taking place and how the house is being provided for. The husbands majorly handle investments and other finance related matters. However, emergency can knock your door uninvited any time.

A close acquaintance of mine, Paula decided to take the plunge two years back. A stay at home mom and manager of her domestic budget, Paula made a firm intention of taking charge of the entire monetary matters parallel to her husband. A wrong investment made on the advice of their relationship manager lead to a huge loss of $20,000 to the family. This served as a wake-up call for her. Perhaps a little vigilance and knowledge about the investment would have averted this loss. Within six months, she converted herself and became the owner of commendable expertise over finances.

After the huge loss that she faced, she braced herself and made a firm determination that her knowledge of finances would extend further than merely spending her husband's earnings. She would also have to look after the matter with more caution. The first step towards this was to enroll her name for an online personal finance course. This helped her learn the basics of finance which including knowledge about investments, banking, taxation, insurance, debit and credit system etc. In a reasonable period, Paula grasped the crux of all the matters.

In addition to above, she also replaced her love for novel reading by reading more of finance related books. Her bookracks now have them neatly shelved and she gladly suggests homemakers a read. Reading has no limit. She spread her wings and absorbed knowledge from personal finance magazines and economic newspapers.

Her taste in television was modified as well. She no longer engaged herself in entertainment channels, rather switched to business channels. Moreover, she got talking to an independent financial advisor who over the time became her guide and a major stepping-stone to attain higher levels. On the advice of her mentor, she attended various workshops and seminars in the city.

Paula is now more aware and vigilant. She has an eye over the entire finances of her house's budget, investments and securities. She knows that the situation of economy, share market, investment climate and policies are forever fluctuating. There will both be fair weather as well as cloudy days. If one wants to secure their future and always have enough at hand to satisfy the needs of the hour, one has to act when the time is right.

Opportunities come and go; wise is the one who makes the most out of it. The weekly or quarterly business releases besides updating you with the current affairs, also allow you to grasp a deep analysis of money matters, read thoughts of financial experts, give you reviews and compare various products, update you with real estate and tell you about the giants in the market. In keeping at par with them, you get a good idea of which baskets you should put your eggs in - that is where you could invest to get better returns.

Apart from everything else, internet is the warehouse of all information. If used in the correct manner, it can be the greatest asset for you to learn everything from the basics up to the professional levels of finance. A good knowledge base will protect you from frauds and scams. You become smarter and better equipped to differentiate between good and bad investments. Moreover, you ensure that all your loans, insurance, taxes and credits are looked after systematically. This not only gives you the assurance of being secure but also helps you build a better future for yourself and your family.

Do not underestimate your skills and power. No matter how alien this area might seem to be from your vision, it is only a matter of taking the first step. Knowledge never goes wasted, especially in money matters. It will forever be your best companion to sail you through the financial crisis. It is never too late to learn and at the end of it, you will stand strong as a prudent woman. Paula is no superwoman. She is there in you, me and every other woman who is the manager of her house.

Education, financial status, age and learning skill are immaterial. All that matters is perseverance and sincerity. We are not aiming to be a professional financer; we are merely aiming at being prudent and wise. Take baby steps and soon you will be where Paula is today!

Chapter 22: Consolidation

Many people hear about consolidation, or consolidation loans but don't know what they are. Your local bank offers them and it can really make a difference in your life.

Let's say you have 3 loans, all for $10,000 and at 10% annual interest (I'm using easy math for this example and not using compounding interest):

Debt #1 $10,000 @10% annual interest= $10,000 loan + $1,000 interest per year= $11,000

Debt #2 $10,000 @10% annual interest= $10,000 loan + $1,000 interest per year= $11,000

Debt #3 $10,000 @ 10% annual interest= $10,000 loan + $1,000 interest per year= $11,000

So if you added all this together, in a year $30,000 loans cost you $3,000 per year in interest.

But what if your bank offered you a loan to pay off your $30,000 in loans at an interest rate that was less than 10%? They would consolidate all three of those debts into one big debt, or consolidate them. Why would your bank do this you ask? Because chances are you don't have all 3 of the loans above with the same bank. One debt may be a student loan, one may be a credit card and the other is a line of credit, all with different lenders. By consolidating, your bank would get ALL that business.

So you get the guts to approach your bank. Go in and tell them you're a client of this bank and you'd like to meet with a personal banker. Then tell the personal banker: "I have $30,000 in debt and I want to consolidate it to one loan". In a matter of minutes, they may say "OK, but the interest rate is 8%".

Quick math: consolidation loan for $30,000 @ 8% annual interest rate: $2400 per year in interest! This immediately saves you $600/ year ($50/month). In fact, it's probably better than that- now, you have to do less work because you only need to make one payment per month instead of 3!

For many, the benefits of consolidation loans is psychological. Part of the reason you likely purchased this e-book is because you feel like you aren't in control of your finances because you have money going of your accounts everywhere. By consolidating, you are wrapping up all those "loose ends" into one package that you pay once per month. It's a much easier way to live and lets you forget about the finances while you focus on more important things.

The Budget Itself

You made it, which means you've already tried to lower your finances by either getting rid of money wasters or consolidated some loans. Or, at least considered ways to lower your finances (you promised me, remember?).

As I mentioned at the start, this budget is not about tracking every item you buy. It's not about carrying around a book or spreadsheet. It's about being realistic, and sustainability.

Sustainability means that you can manage your finances on a daily or weekly basis and keep it up forever. Carrying around a notepad or tracking every purchase on your phone is crazy.

KEY: This simple budget was designed for you to look at every paycheck. If done properly, that is likely the only time you will need to look at it until the next paycheck.

For the sake of simplicity, in the examples below let's determine that you get paid on a monthly basis. The reality is that you are likely paid more frequently (bi-weekly, weekly).

Below, I've given an example of something you can realistically create in Microsoft Excel (or on a sheet of paper if you want). There are no fancy formulas or magic, this is as simple as it needs to be. You should have one of these tables for each pay period. So if you are paid once per week, you'll require 4 of these. If you are paid once per month, you only need one like below:

	Pay date- MONTHLY
Total Pay	$ 1,000
Mortgage	$200
Utilities	$ 75
Phone	$ 75
Gym	$ 50
Groceries	$100
Debt	$200

Car loan	$ 50
Investment	$ 50
Guilt Free $	$200

Let's review each row:

Total Pay: What is your paycheck amount? Put it here.

Mortgage/ Rent: Put in your mortgage amount. Let's say your monthly mortgage/ rent payment is $200, put it in.

Utilities: typically these are extra if you own your home, but may be included in some rent.

Phone: same as above

Gym: same as above

Groceries: This is totally up to you. Keep an eye on how much your groceries cost you and put a **realistic number** here. As well, you need to account for ALL YOUR groceries, not just the ones you do on Saturday. You need to capture the little shops you do on Sunday and Wednesday too. Be honest, what is it costing you in a week?

Debt: Did you consolidate your loans for $200/month? If so that is your debt amount. If you have multiple debts to pay, put the total here. Remember to include any debt/charges that is also coming out of your account, like overdraft charges or monthly bank fees.

Car loan: put all costs associated with your car (if not captured in other buckets). This could include car loan, insurance, gas, repairs

Investment: this is optional but if you want to invest money in retirement savings, the stock market or a savings account, put it in.

The above are simply examples of some of the most common larger expenses. You have may have other expenses that I did not capture but be sure to add them in. The above expenses are the "fixed" expenses that you have monthly. Things like buying lunch, coffee and oil changes do not need to be captured.

Regardless, it all comes down to this: I have a formula in here that takes your "pay" and subtracts all the "bills" and gives you the "guilt free $" in this cell. This is the money you have to spend whatever way you want until your next pay.

The key is to take the guilt free money out of the bank and use that money to pay for everything with that cash. Why? Remember in the introduction when I mentioned about how you had to go to a bank teller 30 years ago to withdraw money? And how there is some accountability by having to physically parting with your money? This is why. Having the cash in hand and watching it disappear also makes you think twice about some of your purchases (do I really need this?), instead of just using your plastic cards without thinking of the implications.

That guilt free money you have is yours to spend on whatever you want, whenever you want. Drink fancy coffee all you want. But that cash in hand needs to last until your next paycheck!

NOTE: If the guilt free $ number is negative, it means that you need to fix some of your everyday spending because you are spending more than you are making. If it is negative, you have two options: spend less or earn more. If this is an isolated situation (for example, you had a hefty repair bill for your car one week that you don't expect to have again), then you should be OK. However, if you are always overspending you need to adjust your lifestyle in some way or the situation will quickly spiral out of control. I would suggest you work with a local financial advisor to develop a plan. The key here is to accept that you are not making your finances work and get some advice before it gets worse (because it will).

Chapter 23: Creating Your Own Budgeting System

When budgeting, you are balancing between your essential needs, your wants and your financial goals. Here are the steps on how you can achieve this balance:

Step 1: Identify your financial priorities

The first step requires you to list all the things that you want in your life that requires a financial commitment. To do this, you need to anticipate future financial needs.

Identifying future financial needs

Before you can start a budget plan, you need to think of your life goals. This is not a very difficult task for most people. We all know what we want to buy if we had some extra money. Some of us want to travel around the world for example, while others just want to buy items that bring them comfort in their own homes.

When we talk about goals in this chapter however, we are not talking about consumer products or entertaining services. We are talking about important life milestones that require money. Buying a house, for instance, is a worthwhile goal. Everybody wants his or her own home. The urgency becomes even greater when you are planning to have a family. You need a home where your family can grow.

A person with no insight will not think of this problem until it is urgent. A wiser person would anticipate this future need and prepare for it financially when he still has a lot of time. You need to think of your future financial needs right after this paragraph. You need to list them all down and put them in order according to their importance.

Adding your passion in the list

Life would be dull if we only worked for what we need. The mind needs a little excitement every now and then. If we think life is exciting, we are more motivated to work.

This is where your passions come in. Aside from your needs, you also need to provide funds for your passions. If you love travelling, you can still do it even if you are following a budget, as long as it is planned and your income justifies such trips.

You should take this time to think of the few luxuries that you will allow yourself and your loved ones to enjoy. You need to have the discipline not to overdo these luxuries. You should only do them to re-motivate yourself and the other members of your family to continue saving.

Step 2: Set the right amount of money for your needs and wants

Now that you know what you need to save for, you need to make a monthly expenses list. When making your list, you need to divide all your expenses into categories. Here are some of the common expense categories:

Food

Utility bills

Transportation expenses

Toiletries, laundry and other home maintenance expenses

These are the expenses common to all adults. Some people however, have other expense categories in their lives. Here are some examples:

Kids' needs

Sports and fitness

Pets

In some months, you will also need to spend money on additional important things. If you have a new job for example, you may need new clothes that will make you fit in. If this is the case, you may need to include a clothes budget for that month. For the holidays, you will also need to include gifts and holiday food categories. By including these seasonal expenses, you will be prepared financially for all of them.

You should also make special categories for specific types of expenses that you wish to keep track of. If you are guilty of spending too much on eating out for example, you may need to cut back on this category. However, we usually include this category with food expenses. To keep track of your total dining-out expenses, you need to make a special category for it and separate it from the food category.

After listing all your expense categories, you need to know how much money each category needs every month. The amount that you should set aside for food for example, depends on the number of people in your family. You need to set fixed amounts for these categories.

You should also anticipate the amount that you need to spend on categories that do not have a fixed price. Your electricity bill for example, varies every month. You need to prepare for the ups and downs of these types of expenses.

Employing a budgeting rule

Aside from the strategies discussed above, you can also apply a budgeting rule to make sure that you do not overspend every month. Here are some of them:

80-10-10 Rule

The 80-10-10 rule is the easiest one to follow. This rule generally means that you spend 80% of your net income on your needs and wants. 10% of your income should go to charity while the last 10% should go to your savings. The rule allows you to share your income with your community while still saving for your long term goals.

60-10-30 Rule

This rule is stricter than the one above. You can use it if you can live comfortably with 60% of your net income. 10% still goes to charity and the 30% goes to your savings. By saving a bigger part of your income, you will be able to reach your financial goals faster.

50% Rule

You should use this rule when you have debts to pay or when there is an urgent short-term goal that you need to reach. In this budgeting rule, you try to make all your needs and wants fit with only 50% of your net income. The other 50% is allocated to your savings. If your needs and wants still go beyond your 50% of your income, you need to cut back on some less important expense categories.

Step 3: Adjust your lifestyle and goals according to your income level

At this point, you already know about the things that you need to spend on right now and the future financial commitments that you need to save for. By now, you should already know if your monthly income would allow you to fund your lifestyle and save for your future financial goals.

If you are one of the lucky ones, there may be some excess money left after all your expenses and savings. For most people however, the income they bring in will not be enough to fund their current lifestyle and save for big goals at the same time. If you have the same experience, you should consider readjusting some areas of your life.

You should first check some of the categories that you listed above and the corresponding amount allocated for these funds. You should identify areas where you can cut back so that you will have more money for savings.

Increase your income

If your income is low, no amount of cutbacks will allow you to save. If you still cannot save after serious cutbacks in all your spending categories, you should find opportunities that will increase your income. If your goals require a large amount of money and you only have a short period to save for it, you also need to take this approach.

Step 4: Allocate your money as soon as you receive it

When your income arrives, the first thing that you need to do is to distribute them properly. The first allocation should go to your savings. By setting money aside as soon as you receive them, you will not be tempted to spend too much on groceries or shopping.

The next categories that you need to allocate for are your basic needs, important utility bills and other important payments. You should not neglect these areas because it is very inconvenient if you miss these payments.

The next area that you need to allocate for is your basic needs. You need to set money aside for food and groceries.

The amount left should be distributed to all the other important expenses that you have listed. If there is still some left after allocating your money, you may spend some part of it for your entertainment or your passions. You may also allocate the money for next month's expenses.

If you receive extra amounts, you have a choice to add it to your savings or to spend it for things and experiences that bring short-term happiness. We recommend that you save it for your goals. The more money you save, the faster you will reach your financial goals.

Step 5: Track your money

As mentioned in the previous chapters, you need to be aware of where your money is going. Money flows in and out of your budget fund. You should make sure that more money goes in than out. To be able to know where your money is going, you need to take note of where every penny is going.

By tracking your money, you will be able to make sure that you are following your planned budget. If you notice that you are spending too fast in the food category for example, you could take measures that will allow you to keep your food expenses low.

To be able to track your money easily, you need a tool that you are familiar with. Here are some of the common tools used by expert budgeters:

1. Notebook and ledger

The easiest tool to use is a notebook that will serve as a logbook where you place all of your expenses for the day. It needs to be small enough that you can carry around. Before the day ends, you should transfer your records to a bigger ledger. You can consult your ledger to analyze your spending habits.

2. Smartphone app

If you are a smartphone user, there are free apps that will allow you to replace the notebook system. Every time you spend, you can just bring out your smart phone and list your expenses. You need to make this activity a habit every time you spend. This is a better option than a notebook because we bring our phone everywhere we go. Unlike the notebook, the app does not become full easily. If it becomes full, you only need to uninstall the app and reinstall it to wipe past records away.

There are premium apps available that provide these types of services but if you do not have the budget, there are also free apps that offer limited features. For most people, the features of the free apps are enough to keep a daily, weekly and monthly record of their expenses.

3. Spreadsheet

Instead of a ledger, you should use a spreadsheet file to store all your expense data. If you are familiar with using this type of tool, you will be able to make calculations faster and make fast interpretations of data presented.

You can use Numbers for Mac or Microsoft Excel if you have these programs in your computer. If not, you can also use open source options available for download online. The open source options' features are enough for this purpose.

Tips on tracking your expenses

- Keep track of even the smallest expenses

People who are new to tracking their money tend to neglect the small expenses. You should keep in mind that all the small expenses add up. Over the course of 6 months or a year, these small expenses will add up to a big amount.

- Keep your tracking descriptions accurate

When checking your expenses in, you need to provide all your notes with accurate descriptions. If you make vague descriptions, you may not remember where the payment was made and you may not be able to categorize the expenses properly.

- Keep receipts or notes when you don't have your tracking tools

There are times when your tracking tools are not available. Your phone may be dead or your notebook may be full. That is why you should always ask for a receipt for all your purchases. If a receipt is not available, you should ask for a piece of paper from the payee so that you can make a note of all your expenses. You should place these notes in your wallet and go back to them at the end of the day.

- Check your expenses record every 12 hours

In the beginning, it will be difficult for you to take note of all of your expenses. You may miss some expenses when you are in a hurry. To prevent lapses in recording your expenses, you should set your alarm for 12 hours. When the alarm goes off, you should set aside whatever you are doing and check if your spending records are complete. You will know if you missed to take note of some expenses if there is a discrepancy between your records and the cash left in your wallet.

Here is an example of a successfully planned budget:

Income		Savings	Expenses Categories	
After Tax Employment Income	3000	2000 (50%)	Food/Groceries	300
Passive Income from	1000		Transportation	150

Businesses					
Total:	40 00			Bills	40 0
				Health Expenses	50
				Entertainment	10 0
				Total:	10 00
				Budget for the rest of the month:	10 00

Conclusion

You have now read through all the important steps of the budgeting process and know what to do to make your hard-earned income work for you. Prepare your tailor-made budget and start saving money NOW. Assume control over your finances and get your debt under control. In good time you'll feel more relaxed and ready to deal with anything that life throws at you.

The budgeting process is also not a straight line; sometimes, you will mess up. Don't give up, and think that all hope is lost. Pick yourself up, learn from the mistakes you made, and make the necessary changes to ensure that you are on your way to achieving financial freedom. Remember, "Rome was not built on one day."

www.ingramcontent.com/pod-product-compliance
Lightning Source LLC
Chambersburg PA
CBHW071225210326
41597CB00016B/1957